**CUMBRIA HERITAGE SERVICES**
LIBRARIES

This book is due to be returned on or before the last date above. It
may be renewed by personal application, post or telephone, if not in
demand.

C.L.18

TO URANIA

Selected Poems 1965–1985

JOSEPH BRODSKY

PENGUIN BOOKS

The author wishes to express his gratitude to Miss Ann Kjellberg for her invaluable help in editing this collection

PENGUIN BOOKS

Published by the Penguin Group
Penguin Books Ltd, 27 Wrights Lane, London W8 5TZ, England
Penguin Books USA Inc., 375 Hudson Street, New York, New York 10014, USA
Penguin Books Australia Ltd, Ringwood, Victoria, Australia
Penguin Books Canada Ltd, 10 Alcorn Avenue, Toronto, Ontario, Canada M4V 3B2
Penguin Books (NZ) Ltd, 182–190 Wairau Road, Auckland 10, New Zealand

Penguin Books Ltd, Registered Offices: Harmondsworth, Middlesex, England

Many of these poems were originally published in Russian by Ardis Publishers in *Urania*, 1987, and
Chast'rechi, 1977
This selection of poems in translation first published in the USA by Farrar, Straus & Giroux,
New York, 1988
Published simultaneously in Canada by Collins Publishers, Toronto
First published in Great Britain by Penguin Books 1988
Published simultaneously in hardback by Viking
3 5 7 9 10 8 6 4 2

Acknowledgments are made to *Cross Currents*, *The New York Review of Books*, *The Paris
Review*, *Partisan Review*, *Ploughshares*, *The Times Literary Supplement*, and *Vanity Fair*,
where some of these poems originally appeared in somewhat different form. The
following poems first appeared in *The New Yorker*: "Eclogue IV: Winter", "Sextet", "To
a Friend: In Memoriam", "Galatea Encore", "Kellomäki", "Belfast Tune", "Eclogue V:
Summer", "Polonaise: A Variation", "October Tune", "In Memoriam", and "The Fly" –
all in slightly different form.

Printed in England by Clays Ltd, St Ives plc

Contents

To Urania

May 24, 1980

I have braved, for want of wild beasts, steel cages,
carved my term and nickname on bunks and rafters,
lived by the sea, flashed aces in an oasis,
dined with the-devil-knows-whom, in tails, on truffles.
From the height of a glacier I beheld half a world, the earthly
width. Twice have drowned, thrice let knives rake my nitty-gritty.
Quit the country that bore and nursed me.
Those who forgot me would make a city.
I have waded the steppes that saw yelling Huns in saddles,
worn the clothes nowadays back in fashion in every quarter,
planted rye, tarred the roofs of pigsties and stables,
guzzled everything save dry water.
I've admitted the sentries' third eye into my wet and foul
dreams. Munched the bread of exile: it's stale and warty.
Granted my lungs all sounds except the howl;
switched to a whisper. Now I am forty.
What should I say about life? That it's long and abhors transparence.
Broken eggs make me grieve; the omelette, though, makes me vomit.
Yet until brown clay has been crammed down my larynx,
only gratitude will be gushing from it.

[*1980* / *Translated by the author*]

3

To a Friend: In Memoriam

It's for you whose name's better omitted—since for them it's no
arduous task
to produce you from under the slab—from one more *inconnu*: me,
well, partly
for the same earthly reasons, since they'll scrub you as well off the
cask,
and because I'm up here and, frankly, apart from this paltry
talk of slabs, am too distant for you to distinguish a voice,
an Aesopian chant, in that homeland of bottle-struck livers,
where you fingered your course to the pole in the moist universe
of mean, blabbering squinchers and whispering, innocent beavers;
it's for you, name omitted, the offspring of a widowed conductress,
begot
by the Holy Ghost or by brick courtyard's soot circling all over,
an abductor of books, the sharp pen of the most smashing ode
on the fall of the bard at the feet of the laced Goncharova,
a word-plyer, a liar, a gulper of bright, measly tears,
an adorer of Ingres, of clangoring streetcars, of asphodels' slumbers,
a white-fanged little snake in the tarpaulin-boot colonnade of
gendarmes in full gear,
a monogamous heart and a torso of countless bedchambers—
may you lie, as though wrapped in an Orenburg shawl, in our dry,
brownish mud,
you, a tramper through hell and high water and the meaningless
sentence,
who took life like a bumblebee touching a sun-heated bud
but instead froze to death in the Third Rome's cold-piss-reeking
entrance.
Maybe Nothing has no better gateway indeed than this smelly
shortcut.
Man of sidewalks, you'd say, "This will do," adding, "for the
duration,"
as you drifted along the dark river in your ancient gray, drab
overcoat
whose few buttons alone were what kept you from disintegration.
Gloomy Charon in vain seeks the coin in your tightly shut shell,

4

someone's pipe blows in vain its small tune far above heavy, cumulous
curtains.

With a bow, I bid you this anonymous, muted farewell
from the shores—who knows which? Though for you now it has no
importance.

[*1973 / Translated by the author*]

October Tune

A stuffed quail
on the mantelpiece minds its tail.
The regular chirr of the old clock's healing
in the twilight the rumpled helix.
Through the window, birch candles fail.

For the fourth day the sea hits the dike with its hard horizon.
Put aside the book, take your sewing kit;
patch my clothes without turning the light on:
golden hair
keeps the corner lit.

[*1968 / Translated by the author*]

A Polar Explorer

All the huskies are eaten. There is no space
left in the diary. And the beads of quick
words scatter over his spouse's sepia-shaded face
adding the date in question like a mole to her lovely cheek.
Next, the snapshot of his sister. He doesn't spare his kin:
what's been reached is the highest possible latitude!
And, like the silk stocking of a burlesque half-nude
queen, it climbs up his thigh: gangrene.

[*1977 / Translated by the author*]

Lithuanian Nocturne

To Thomas Venclova

I

Having roughed up the waters,
wind explodes like loud curses from fist-ravaged lips
in the cold superpower's
innards, squeezing trite wobbles
of the do-re-mi from sooted trumpets that lisp.
Nonprincesses and porous
nonfrogs hug the terrain,
and a star shines its mite clouds don't bother to tamper
with. A semblance of face
blots the dark windowpane
like the slap of a downpour.

II

Greetings, Thomas. That's my
specter—having abandoned its frame in a fleabag somewhere
overseas, rowing through
whipped-up thick northern cumulus, thereby
tearing from the New World—which wings homeward,
and this thoroughfare
duly brings him to you.

III

Late Lithuanian dusk.
Folk are scuffling from churches protecting the commas
of their candle flames in trembling brackets of hands;
in the freezing courtyards
chickens peck in the sodden sawdust,
over stubbled Zhemaitija's contours
snow's aswirl like the ashes from burnt-out celestial wards.
From the doors flung askew,
fish soup's odor is oozing. A youngster, half naked,
and a kerchiefed old hag chase a pig to the sty.
And a cart-riding Jew,

8

late for home, drums the village's cobblestone, trying to make it,
yanks the reins hard
and bellows "Gerai!"

IV

Sorry for the invasion.
Take this apparition for, let's
say, an early return of the quote back to its Manifesto's
text: a notch more, say, slurred, and a pitch more alluring
for being away.
Thus don't cross yourself, etc.,
and don't torture gauze curtains: I'll vanish as fast as
roosters herald the day.
Sorry for the intrusion.
Don't reel into a bedroom in fright:
it's just frailty that widens its reach at the cost of state borders.
Like a stone that avenges a well
with its multiple rings,
I buzz over the Baltic, like that ill-fated flight
of Girenas and Darius, the immortals!—
but on less brittle wings.

V

Evening in the Empire,
in a destitute province. A conifer force
wades the Neman and, bristling with darkening lances,
takes old three-storied Kaunas; a blush of remorse
sweeps the stucco as darkness advances,
and the cobblestones glisten like bream in a net.
At the opera, up soars a patterned
curtain, while in an archway the object of passion
gets divided by three, with, I bet,
no leftovers. The dark thrills the calm
tulle. A star, shining in a backwater,
does so all the more brightly: like a card played in suit.
And your delta-like palm
drums the pane, flowing into the outer
dark—a cheerless pursuit.

Every speech after midnight
develops a blind man's technique.
Even "homeland," by touch, feels like Lady Godiva.
Cobweb-shaded, the mikes
of the secret police in a bard's quarters pick
up the mattress's sighs, and the dripping saliva
of the national anthem: the tune that dislikes
using words. Here reticence reigns. Trembling leaves
torn between their reverse and their surface
irritate a lamppost. Spurning loudspeakers, a man
here declares to the world that he lives
by unwittingly crushing an ant,
by faint Morse's
dots of pulse, by the screech of his pen.

That's whence that mealy grain
of your cheeks, your quite addressless, senseless
stare, your lisping, your hair
with its shade of weak colorless tea down the drain;
that's whence, too, one's whole life's honest, hesitant sentence:
a comma-bound affair.
It is thence also its
upward spinoffs: my washed-out appearance
in your windows; uprisings—with threats to invade—
of sharp willow twigs, etc.;
ocean's pages, one's leafings through them in the quest for a period,
a horizon, a fate.

Our cuneiform, Thomas! With my margin-prone
predicates! with your subjects, hearthbound and luckless!
Our inkpot alliance! Its splurge!
Doodling lace, herringbone,
Roman writ *cum* Cyrillic, harking to Magnavox's
ends-*cum*-means demiurge!
Our imprints! In damp twisted sheets
—in that flabby brainlike common cotton—
in our loved ones' soft clay, in our children without us, or

as a bruise that still sits
on the firmament, brought on-
to its cheek by a youngster whose sore
eye was trying to fathom the distance from that
famed Lithuanian inn,
to the multieyed face gazing sideways
like some old squinting Mongol beyond our spiked earthly fence,
poised to put fingers in-
to his mouth—that old wound of your namesake!—to find its
tongue and alter, like seraphs and silence
do, his verbs or their tense.

IX
Thomas, we are alike;
we are, frankly, a double:
your breath
dims the same windowpane that my features befuddle.
We're each other's remote
amalgam underneath,
in a lackluster puddle,
a simultaneous nod.
Twist your lips—I'll reply with the similar grimace of dread.
I'll respond to your yawn with my mouth's gaping mollusc.
I'll cry rivers to your
hundred-watt swollen tear overhead.
We're a mutual threat,
Castor looming through Pollux,
we're a stalemate, no-score,
draw, long shadows' distress
brought to walls by a match that will die in a minute,
echoes tracing in vain the original cry
as small change does its note.
The more life has been ruined, the less
is the chance to distinguish us in it
with an indolent eye.

X
What do specters live by?
By the refuse of dreams,
borders' dross, the chaff of mute odd numbers or even,

for addresses are what makes reality hark
back. A lane gnashes, gumlike, its porches agleam;
like a simpleton's cheese, alleys' yellow is eaten
by the fox of the dark
hours. Avenging its permanence, a
place stuffs time with a tenant, a lodger—
with a life-form, and throws up the latch.
And an epoch away
I still find you in this dog-eared kingdom of cudgel
forests, plains, well-preserving one's features, one's thinking and such,
but above all, the pose:
in her many-miled, damp
hemp nightgown, in her high-voltage curlers,
dormant Mother Lithuania's taking her rest
by the shore, as you're gluing your plump
lips to her bare and colorless
glassy half-liter breast.

XI
There are places in which
things don't change. These are a substitute
for one's memory. These are the acid
triumphs of fixative. There each mile
puts striped bars into focus; one's suit
gravitates to a silhouette, added
to one's thinking. Meanwhile,
soldiers keep growing younger. The past
peers ahead with a wary
eye, well matching the khaki attire of youth,
and one's fate, like a border trespasser, reels fast
into brittle old age with its spittle, its aching, its weary
shuffling down the infinity-reeking night pavements. In truth,
night's the border where reality, like
Tartars, threatens the kingdom
of what has been lived through with a raid, or perhaps vice versa;
where logs
join their trees and split back into logs, where daylight
grabs what night's left unhidden
under tight eyelids' locks.

Midnight. Cries of a jay
sound human and charge Mother Nature
with the crime of thermometers: with zerocide.
His bleak shield thrown away
and sword ditched, Prince Vytautas is ready to venture
our flatulent Baltic, with the Swedes out of sight
but in mind. However, the land
overtakes him, assuming the shape of a lengthy
pier, to catch up with freedom long fled
climbing over flat ladderlike waves. In the end,
the best-built beaver dam in the woods cries a-plenty:
tears gleam silver and lead.

Midnight in a deciduous region,
in a province the shade
of topcoats. Belfries' wedges. A swatch of a cloud
to enshroud a contiguous nation. Below,
haystacks, pastures, a glade
of roof tiles, colonnades, brick, cast-iron; and—proud
in his boots—a by-blow
of the state. Midnight's oxygen gets
flooded with interference, with weather reports, news, and prayers,
with the Vizier of Woes
and his rounded numbers, with anthems, sextets,
jigs, decrees, with anathema-sayers,
banning things no one knows.

A specter wanders in Kaunas. It enters, by chance,
a cathedral. Runs out. Drifts along Laisvis Boulevard. Enters
empty "Tulpe," slumps down on a chair.
Yet the waiter who'd glance
in this corner will spot just white napkins, or embers
of the cabs outside, snowflakes circling—and stare
at the street. You would envy, I think,
me: for invisibility comes into fashion
with the passage of years—as the body's concession to its

soul, as a well-taken hint
of the future, as Paradise's fathom-
like attire, as a drawn-out minus that fits
everyone. For all profit from absence, from stark
nonextension: a mountain, a valley,
a brass pendulum plate with two glimmers to serve,
the Almighty that gazes from stars
downward, mirrors, a squealer,
corridors, you yourself.

XV

A specter loiters about in Kaunas. It is
but your thoughts of me added
to the air, but a vacuum rampant, and not
that tempestuous sermon of social bliss.
So don't envy me at it,
simply note
in this faint apparition a kin
or an aspect of air—like these words, with their fear of the morning,
scattered thinly at midnight by some slurring voice—
a sound more like houseflies
bravely clicking a tin,
and which won't satiate
the new Clio adorning
checkpoint gowns, but in which
ever-naked Urania is to rejoice!
Only she, our Muse
of the point lost in space, our Muse of forgotten
outlines can assess, and in full,
like a miser, the use
of small change, immobility's token
paid for flights of the soul.

XVI

That's whence, Thomas, the pen's
troth to letters. That's what must explain gravitation,
don't you think?
With the roosters' "Time's up,"
that light-entity rends
its light self from its verbs and their tense,

1 4

from its hair-shirted nation,
from—let's loosen the trap—
you: from letters, from pages, from sound's
love for sense, from incorporeality's passion
toward mass, and from freedom's, alas,
love for slavery's haunts—
for the bone, for the flesh, and
for the heart—having thus
liberated itself, that light-entity soars up to ink-
like dark heavenly reaches,
past blind cherubs in niches,
past the bats that won't wink.

XVII

Muse of dots lost in space! Muse of things one makes out
through a telescope only! Muse of subtraction
but without remainders! Of zeroes, in short.
You who order the throat
to avoid lamentation,
not to go overboard,
that is, higher than "la"!
Muse, accept this effect's
little aria sung to the gentle
cause's sensitive ear,
and regard it and its do-re-me-ing tercets
in your rarefied rental
from the viewpoint
of air,
of pure air! Air indeed is the epilogue
for one's retina: nobody stands to inhabit
air! It is our "homeward"! That town
which all syllables long
to return to. No matter how often you grab it,
light or darkness soon darn with their rapid
needles air's eiderdown.

XVIII

Every thing has a limit: the horizon that splits
a round eye; for despair, it is memory; often
it's the hand's fabled reach.

Only sound, Thomas, slips,
specter-like, from the body. An orphan
sound, Thomas, is speech.
Push the lampshade aside, and by staring
straight ahead
you'll see air *en face*:
swarms of those
who have stained it
with their lips before us.

XIX

In the kingdom of air!
In its equality of
gulps of oxygen to our syllables! In the transparent
lumped-like-clouds exhalations of ours! In that
world where, like our dreams haunt the ceiling,
our O's
shape the vault of the palate,
where a star gets its shine from the vat
of the throat! That's how the universe
breathes. And that's what a rooster's sharp yokel
meant by sparing the larynx the draught's dry assaults.
Air, the tongue's running course!
And the firmament's a chorus of highly pitched vocal
atoms, alias souls.

XX

That is why it is pure!
In this world, there is nothing that bleaches
pages better (except
for one's dying) than air.
And the whiter, the emptier, which is
homelike. Muse, may I set
out homeward? To that out-loud
realm where witless Boreas
tramples over the trophies of lips in his flight,
to your grammar without
punctuation, to your Paradise of our alphabets
and tracheas,
to your blackboard in white.

In the sky
far above the Lithuanian hills
something sounding like a prayer
for the whole of mankind, droning cheerlessly, drifts
toward Kurshskaya Point. This is St. Casimir's
and St. Nicholas's mumbling in their unattainable lair
where, minding the passage of darkness, they sift
hours. Muse! from the heights where you
dwell, beyond any creed's stratosphere, from your rarefied ether,
look, I pray you, together
with those two,
after these pacified sunken plains' sullen bard.
Do not let handmade darkness envelop his rafter.
Post your sentinels in his back yard.
Look, Urania, after
both his home and his heart.

[*1974 / Translated by the author*]

Twenty Sonnets to Mary Queen of Scots

Mary, I call them pigs, not Picts, those Scots.
What generation of what clan in tartan
could have foreseen you'd step down from the screen
a statue, and bring life to city gardens—
the Luxembourg, to be precise? I came
here to digest a Paris lunch and stare,
with the dull eyes of a decrepit ram,
at the new gates and into ponds. And here
I met Your Highness. And to mark that meeting
and since "all the dead past now lives anew
in my cold heart," by way of greeting,
I'll stuff the old gun full of classic grape-
shot, squandering what remains of Russian speech
on your pale shoulders and your paler nape.

The war to end all wars produced ground zero.
The frying pan missed fat that missed pork chops.
Mary, I was a boy then, and saw Zarah
Leander approach the scaffold, clippety-clop.
Whatever you may say, the axman's blade
equates the ditches to the lofty reaches
(cf., our luminary rising late).
We all came to the surface from the pictures,
but something calls us, at the hour of gloom,
back to the Spartacus, whose plushy womb
is cozier than a European evening.
There the stars hang, the grandest a brunette;
there are two features, everybody queuing,
and not an empty seat, I bet.

I, who have traveled half my earthly road,
make my appearance in the Luxembourg
and contemplate the petrified gray curls
of thinkers and of scribblers. Gents and broads

are strolling to and fro; a whiskered
blue copper glistens from the thicket;
the fountain purrs, the children laugh,
and not a soul to greet with "Bugger off."
And you, untiring, Mary, stand and stand,
in the stone garland of your girl friends—stunned
French queens of once-upon-has-been,
in silence, with a sparrow in your hair.
You'd think the garden was a cross between
the Pantheon and *Déjeuner sur l'herbe.*

IV

The beauty whom I later loved—quite likely
more tenderly than you loved Bothwell—had
some features similar to yours ("My God,"
I automatically whisper, lately
recalling them). Moreover, we,
like you, did not make a happy pair.
Wearing a mackintosh, she went off somewhere.
To sidestep the straight line of destiny,

I cut across another line—whose edge
is sharper than a knife blade: the horizon,
Mary. With neck above that thing outstretched—
not for the oxygen but the breathtaking poison
that bursts my Adam's apple with a squeal—
the larynx's sort of grateful for the deal.

V

The number of your lovers, Mary, went
beyond the figure three, four, twenty, twent-
y-five. A crown, alas, gets dented, bent,
or lost between the sheets with some odd gent.
That's why a monarchy comes to an end
while a republic may be permanent
(see ancient pillars or a monument).
And your Scots barons neither couldn't, nor can't
think otherwise. They wouldn't relent
in pressing their quite sordid argument—
that is, that they, your Scottish lords, can't see

what makes a throne so different from a cot.
O *rara avis* of your century!
To your compatriots you were a slut.

VI

I loved you. And my love of you (it seems,
it's only pain) still stabs me through the brain.
The whole thing's shattered into smithereens.
I tried to shoot myself—using a gun
is not so simple. And the temples: which one,
the right or left? Reflection, not the twitching,
kept me from acting. Jesus, what a mess!
I loved you with such strength, such hopelessness!
May God send you in others—not a chance!
He, capable of many things at once,
won't—citing Parmenides—reinspire
the bloodstream fire, the bone-crushing creeps,
which melt the lead in fillings with desire
to touch—"your hips," I must delete—your lips.

VII

Paris is still the same. The Place des Vosges
is still, as once it was (don't worry), square.
The Seine has not run backward to its source.
The Boulevard Raspail is still as fair.
As for the new, there's music now for free,
a tower to make you feel you're just a fly,
no lack of people whom it's nice to see,
provided you're the first to blurt "How's life?"

Paris by night, a restaurant . . . What chic
in words like these—a treat for vocal cords.
And in comes *eine kleine nachtmuzhik*,
an ugly cretin in a Russian shirt.
Café. Boulevard. The girlfriend in a swoon.
The General-Secretary's-coma moon.

VIII

In my decline, in a land beyond the seas
(discovered in Your Highness's time, methinks),

splitting my animated frame between
a stove and a divan with busted springs,
I muse how just a few words would have been
enough for us, if fate had crossed our paths:
you would have simply called me "dear Ivan,"
and I'd have answered with one word, "Alas."

Scotland would have been our mattress then.
I'd have displayed you to the haughty Slavs.
Port Glasgow would have seen a caravan
of satins, Russian cakes, and shoes of bast
come sailing in. And we'd have met our fate
together. Severed by a wooden blade.

IX

A plain. Alarum. Enter two. The clash
of battle. "Who are you?" "And you yourself?"
"Us? we are Protestants, we don't observe . . ."
"And we are Catholics." "Ah, bloody Papists!" Crash!
And then the corpses lie about like trash,
the endless din of crows' first-come-first-served.
And later—winter, sleigh rides through the slush.
A shawl from Persia. "Persia! Ah! what nerve!"
"A land where peacocks make their peahens blush."
"Yet even there a queen at night can shush
her shah." "Or mate him, playing chess up north
in a cute Hollywood-style modest castle." Slash:
a plain again. Time: midnight. Enter two.
And drown you with their wolfish who-is-who.

X

An autumn evening. All but with the Muse.
Alas, not heeding the relentless lyre.
That's nothing new. On evenings such as these
you'd play for kicks even the army choir.
Becoming yesterday, today won't use
new sheets of paper, pen, or oatmeal's mire
and let the crippled Hamburg cooper cruise
night skies at length. About the secondhand,
soiled, scratched, or badly dented items:

time seems a teeny bit more confident
than fresh tomatoes, and at least won't bite them.
The door may creak: death, having failed to knock,
will stand before you in her moth-holed frock.

XI

A clang of shears, a momentary chill.
Fate, envying the sheepfolk for their wool,
knocks off our crowns and bridal wreaths at will—
quite indiscriminately. And the heads as well.
Farewell, young dudes, their proud dads, their ill-
kept promises, divorces, all to hell.
The brain's like a skyscraper in whose still
tight shell each cell ignores another cell.
That's how the twins in distant Siam swill
their booze: one does it, but they both feel swell.
No one has shouted to you, "Watch out!"
Nor did you, Mary, know enough to shout,
"I am alone"—while boring God and pew
with Latin pleas—"There are a lot of you!"

XII

What is it that makes History? Well, bodies.
And Art?—a body that has lost its head.
Take Schiller, say. Young Friedrich served his notice
to History. You never dreamt, I bet,
a Jerry'd get, out of the blue, so hot as
to resurrect the ancient case, long dead.
It's not his business to discuss your quotas:
who had you or who didn't in a bed.

But then, perhaps, like every other Hans,
our Fritz was simply frightened of the ax.
And secondly, dear Mary, let me stress:
there's nothing, barring Art, sublunar creatures
can use to comprehend your gorgeous features.
Leave History to Good Queen Bess.

A ram shakes out his ringlets, alias fleece,
inhaling lazily the scent of hay.
All round are standing Glencorns, Douglases,
et al. These were the words they spoke that day:
"They have cut off her head." "They have, alas."
"Just think what those in gay Paree will say."
"The French? About the head of some poor lass?
Now, were it aimed above the knee, they may . . ."
"She's not a man, though. Came out in her shift."
"That's not enough to rest one's case upon . . ."
"You could see through it. Shameless!" "What of it?
Could be she's got no gown for putting on."
"Yeah, she's no Russian. 'Ivanov,' I mean,
suggests a wench whichever case it's in."

Love is more powerful than separation, but
the latter is more lasting. Plus, the greater
the statue, the more palpably it ain't her.
Her voice, her wits, smell, finally, are cut
off. While one blames it on the granite that
you won't kick up your legs to starry heights, for
so many fingers' failure to decipher
your petticoats, one has to punish but

one's awkward self. It's not 'cause so much blood
and so much water—equally blue—
have flowed under the bridge, but since the brass
bed screams at night under a lonely lad,
I'd have erected, too, a stone for you,
but I would cut it in transparent glass.

Your ruin, Mary, wasn't the grooms who'd got
no carpenters to raise the roofbeams higher
in that small chamber where they bravely fought;
nor was it that smart ink, which only fire
makes visible (and you were never caught);

nor that Elizabeth loved England's plot
indeed more than you did your Scottish shire
(which is the truth, though some will cry it's not);
nor those good tunes the Spaniard would admire,
especially coming from a royal throat;
no, what they killed you for—let's clear the mire—
was something to which they, in those old days,
could see no end: the beauty of your face.

XVI

As corners vanish, softened by the dark,
a square, too, gradually becomes a sphere.
The crimson wood, like a doused fire,
peers into night with all its pores of bark,
in silence, listening to cranes up there.
Triggered by swishing leaves, a setter's bark
flies to the seven stars that mutely stare
on withered winter crops, forlorn and stark.

How few among those things that once could cause
a tear of pleasure have survived the passage
into the humus shade, how little stays.
The fountain pen now has to stick to those
that failed to heed another season's message,
to squeak and echo "Melancholy Days."

XVII

The thing that dragged from English mouths a shout
of wonderment, that still impels
my own two lips—keen for a lipsticked pout—
to use foul epithets, that rang the bells
for Philip, sending his great painter out
and ordering the great Armada sail;
it was—it seems I can't complete the big
buildup of phrases—well, your wig,
red, lying fallen from your fallen (wow,
that's rich!) head, was your one and only bow
to any audience (with no free seat),
and though it didn't cause a major fight

2 4

among spectators, it was such a sight
it brought your enemies to their cold feet.

XVIII

To one whose mouth has said farewell to you,
not just to anyone, isn't it all the same,
whatever tasteless crusts he has to chew
in years to come? I'll wager you became
accustomed to the lack of do-re-mi.
And if you didn't, don't be cross with me:
ratlike the tongue goes scurrying through a mound
of rubbish, seeking treasure left behind.

Forgive me then, fair idol on the lawn.
Yes, separation is no fool, to own
them measly peanuts. For between us lie
eternity and ocean. Literally.
Plus Russian censorship, in case you ask.
They could have done the job without an ax.

XIX

The Scots have wool now, Mary (and it all
looks spick-and-span like from the cleaners, great).
At six o'clock life judders to a stall,
leaving no mark upon the sunset's plate.
The lakes—unnumbered as in days gone by—
have spawned strange monsters (serpentine and frisky),
and soon they'll have their private oil supply,
Scotch oil, to go in bottles meant for whiskey.
It looks like Scotland got along just fine
without you, and England too, one hears.
And you in this *jardin* of French design
don't look the madcap of those yesteryears.
And there are dames through whose silk folds I'd rummage—
but the comparison would do you damage.

XX

With simple pen (rebellious, not true!)
I've sung this meeting under foreign eaves

with her who taught me from the screen a few
facts of the heart on '48's cold eves.

Now judge, ye of all races and beliefs:
(a) if he learned his lessons (one or two),
(b) the new setting where a Russian lives,
(c) moments of grammatical voodoo.

Nepal's far capital is Katmandu.

Being absolute, the arbitrary gives
a helping hand to everything we do.

Leading the life I lead, I am grateful to
the sheaf of previously snow-white leaves
of paper, rolled for simply blowing through.

[*1974 / Translated by Peter France and the author*]

North Baltic

To C.H.

When a blizzard powders the harbor, when the creaking pine
leaves in the air an imprint deeper than a sled's steel runner,
what degree of blueness can be gained by an eye? What sign
language can sprout from a chary manner?
Falling out of sight, the outside world
makes a face its hostage: pale, plain, snowbound.
Thus a mollusc stays phosphorescent at the ocean's floor
and thus silence absorbs all speeds of sound.
Thus a match is enough to set a stove aglow;
thus a grandfather clock, a heartbeat's brother,
having stopped this side of the sea, still tick-tocks to show
time at the other.

[*1975 / Translated by the author*]

The Berlin Wall Tune

To Peter Viereck

This is the house destroyed by Jack.
    This is the spot where the rumpled buck
stops, and where Hans gets killed.
    This is the wall that Ivan built.

This is the wall that Ivan built.
    Yet trying to quell his sense of guilt,
he built it with modest gray concrete,
    and the booby traps look discreet.

Under this wall that (a) bores, (b) scares,
    barbed-wire meshes lie flat like skeins
of your granny's darnings (her chair still rocks!).
    But the voltage's too high for socks.

Beyond this wall throbs a local flag
    against whose yellow, red, and black
Compass and Hammer proclaim the true
    Masonic dream's breakthrough.

The border guards patiently in their nest
    through binoculars scan the West
and the East; and they like both views
    devoid, as it were, of Jews.

Those who are seen here, thought of, felt,
    are kept on a leash by the sense of Geld
or by a stronger Marxist urge.
    The wall won't let them merge.

Come to this wall if you hate your place
    and face a sample of cosmic space
where no life forms can exist at all
    and objects may only fall.

Come to this scornful of peace and war,
    petrified version of either/or
meandering through these bleak parts which act
    like your mirror, cracked.

Dull is the day here. In the night
    searchlights illuminate the blight
making sure that if someone screams,
    it's not due to bad dreams.

For dreams here aren't bad: just wet with blood
    of one of your like who's left his pad
to ramble at will; and in his head
    dreams are replaced with lead.

Given that, it's only time
    who has guts enough to commit the crime
of passing this place back and forth on foot:
    at pendulums they don't shoot.

That's why this site will see many moons
    while couples lie in their beds like spoons,
while the rich are wondering what they wish
    and single girls eat quiche.

Come to this wall that beats other walls:
    Roman, Chinese, whose worn-down, false
molars envy steel fangs that flash,
    scrubbed of thy neighbor's flesh.

A bird may twitter a better song.
    But should you consider abortion wrong
or that the quacks ask too high a fee,
    come to this wall, and see.

[*1980*]

Dutch Mistress

A hotel in whose ledgers departures are more prominent than arrivals.
With wet Koh-i-noors the October rain
strokes what's left of the naked brain.
In this country laid flat for the sake of rivers,
beer smells of Germany and seagulls are
in the air like a page's soiled corners.
Morning enters the premises with a coroner's
punctuality, puts its ear
to the ribs of a cold radiator, detects sub-zero:
the afterlife has to start somewhere.
Correspondingly, the angelic curls
grow more blond, the skin gains its distant, lordly
white, while the bedding already coils
desperately in the basement laundry.

[*1981*]

Allenby Road

At sunset, when the paralyzed street gives up
hope of hearing an ambulance, finally settling for
strolling Chinamen, while the elms imitate a map
of a khaki-clad country that lulls its foe,
life is gradually getting myopic, spliced,
aquiline, geometrical, free of gloss
or detail—be it cornices, doorknobs, Christ—
stressing silhouettes: chimneys, rooftops, a cross.
And your closing the shutters unleashes the domino
theory; for no matter what size a lump
melts in your throat, the future snowballs each "no"
to coin a profile by the burning lamp.
Neither because there is a lot of guilt
nor because local prices are somewhat steep,
nobody picks this brick pocket filled
with change that barely buys some sleep.

[*1981*]

The Fifth Anniversary

June 4, 1977

A falling star, or worse, a planet (true or bogus)
might thrill your idle eye with its quick hocus-pocus.
Look, look then at that locus that's better out of focus.

.   .   .

There frowning forests stand decked out in rags and tatters.
Departing from point A, a train there bravely scatters
its wheels toward point B. Which station hardly matters.

There causes and effects are drowned in murky waters.
One's corpse there lies unseen; so does, of course, one's foetus.
It's different with birds; but eggs don't beg for photos.

At dusk a Steinway grand twangs out a thin B-minor.
There musty jackets hang, the moth their redesigner.
On rocks, enchanted oaks nod to a passing liner.

.   .   .

There a puddle in the yard is neither round nor square.
There single mothers pot their daughters in day care.
A boisterous mountain stream strives for the third shore there.

A kid stares down his dad there all the way to breeches.
There rockets carry up crafts filled with barking bitches
plus officers whose pay suggests the upper reaches.

There weeds submit to green: a sort of common harness.
A principle of sound owes to a bee that's harmless.
A copy, sparing its original, stays armless.

.   .   .

In winter, Arctic winds shake parks to herald foul days,
and radiators which absorb the dust in hallways
possess more ribs than girls. A freezing man, though, always

prefers the former, which, in turn, appear more eager.
At tea, a candy hurts a tooth that's scarcely bigger.
A sleeping guard enjoys wet dreams and pulls the trigger.

There on a rainy day a sulphur match looks shocking.
They say, "It's only us," with rotten smirks while knocking.
There fish scales shine with tin, in lakes where fish are soaking.

      .   .   .

There having voted yes, they sob in toilet corners.
There icons in the church turn black from incense burners.
The army shows who's who to folks across the borders.

There orchards burst in view, thus aping epic horsemen.
The liquor store's long queue needs only you to worsen.
Behind you and in front, you find the same stiff person.

There snatches of old tunes hang in the air they brighten
Wheat left the zeal of state: it's a collector's item.
There martens quit the woods, whose branches fail to hide them.

      .   .   .

There even when you lie flat on a sheet of cotton,
your shadow dwarfs a palm in Palestine, begotten
most likely in a dream. There deserts lie well-trodden

by sugar bowls' houseflies, which trek on foot, old-style.
There under rakish roofs small windows squint hostile.
The world map is replaced there by a large Holstein

a-mooing on a hill, awash in sunset's slobber.
There steel mills far away belch heavy smoke and clobber,
though no one needs all that; no matter drunk or sober.

      .   .   .

There owls hoot late at night on matters vain and ashen.
No leader seems quite fit to stop green leaves' ovation.
There brain folds spurn straight thought for being out of fashion.

The hammer-hugging sickle there adorns the banner.
But nails are not struck home and weeds submerge the planner:
into the Great Machine someone has lobbed a spanner.

Apart from these, there are no enigmas, signs in heavens.
The landscape's dull, and its horizon's notched with cave-ins.
There gray is all the rage—the tint of time and cabins.

.   .   .

I grew up in those parts. I used to share a cigarette
with their most gifted bard. Was kept, a guilty secret,
in cells. Admired lead skies, as well as windswept liquid.

There I thought I would die. From boredom or from terror.
If not in friendly arms, then at their hands. But there or
somewhere nearby. Today I see my error.

I see that I was wrong. For on a stage the actor
means less than backdrops do. Space is a greater factor
than horsemen. Space won't tell the front legs from the back two.

.   .   .

Well, I'm no longer there. The sense of loss, as much as
this was indeed a loss, is best displayed by statues
in galleries, or by their vases' mute "Don't touch us."

The place sustained this loss. Some moss combined with lichen,
encountering the hole I've made, will quickly stitch it.
A connoisseur of hues won't tell you later which one

is missing. This feels odd but constitutes a variant.
It would be odder still to lie there low and ironed
or play a warrior valiant and nudge an aging tyrant.

.   .   .

So I'm no longer there. All things have rules to reckon.
I never liked fat cats, and never kissed an icon.
And on a certain bridge, a black cast-iron Gorgon

seemed in those parts to me the truth's most honest version.
So later having met her in gigantic person,
I haven't turned to stone and let my lumpy portion

of savage screams go stale. I hear the Muse's prattle.
I sense the thread within strained by the Parcae's shuttle:
the spheres still tolerate my CO_2 life rattle,

.   .   .

as my free-flapping tongue, a glutton for clear lyric
sends its Cyrillic thanks into the blue acrylic
to fate—since fate can grasp the meaning in Cyrillic

as well. I face pure space, which tolerates no columns
nor torsos of Apollos, nor pyramids, nor chorus.
There, it appears, I need no guide; at least, it follows.

Scratch on, my clawlike pen, my pilgrim staff, my salvage!
Don't rush our shuffling words: the age wheel-deep in garbage
won't overtake us and won't grab you, barefoot savage.

.   .   .

This won't be heard up North, nor where hot sands hug cactus.
I don't know anymore what earth will nurse my carcass.
Scratch on, my pen: let's mark the white the way it marks us.

[*1977 / Translated by the author*]

Polonaise: A Variation

To Z.K.

I

Autumn in your hemisphere whoops cranes and owls.
A lean nation's frontier slips off like a loosened harness.
And though windows aren't sealed yet, your camisole's
cleavage adds to the shadows the parlor harvests.
As the lamps flare up, one may well denounce
one's own curves as jarring the jigsaw puzzle
of the rooms whose air savors every ounce
pecked by Frederyk's keyboard-bedeviled nozzle.
In the full moon, the stubble gets lavished with
nobody's silver by sloughy waters.
Roll on your side, and the dreams will blitz
out of the wall like those fabled warriors
heading east, through your yard, to dislodge the siege
of tall hemp. Still, their hauberks won't hide their tatters.
Yet, since they look alike, you, by getting hitched
only once, let an army across your mattress.

II

Reddish tiles of the homestead, and the yellow shade
of its stuccoed dwellings, beset with shingles.
Either cartwheels are craving an oval shape
or the mare's hoof, hitting the cow-moon, shimmies,
and slumped haystacks flash by. Alders, nothing-clad,
in their basket carry away the river.
And the leaden plow in the furrowed clouds
bodes no good to gray winter crops racked with fever.
To your woolen stockings and linen hem
burdocks cling like nobody's child that loses
in the end its grip. And space is stitched firm
with the threadbare rain, and Copernicus turns out useless.
Still, the iris gleams, and the milky tint,
with those scattered birthmarks, your dress effaces.
Long a silhouette to yourself, you won't
fall into anyone's fond embraces.

I admit that one's love should be greater, more
pure. That one could, like the son of Cronus,
size up the darkness, perfect its lore,
and drop, unnoticed, within your contours.
That one could reconstruct, pore by pore, your true
looks, with idle atoms and mental power;
or just peer at the mirror and state that you
are me: for whom do we love but our-
selves? Yet chalk one up for Fate: your watch
may be running behind, for in our future
already that bomb has exploded which
leaves intact only the furniture.
Does it really matter who's run away from whom?
Neither time nor space is matchmaking for us
who took full advantage of sampling some
of those ages to come, and whatever follows.

[*1981 / Translated by the author*]

The New Jules Verne

To Lev and Nina Loseff

I

A perfect line of horizon. Without a blot. A swanky
clipper, whose Franz Liszt profile keeps stabbing
the waves. Tight cables are creaking. A naked monkey
with a scream leaps out of the naturalist's hot cabin.

Dolphins bounce along. As someone remarked somewhere,
only bottles in bars experience no seasickness.
A squall tears off the punch line of a joke, and the captain's bare
fists in a flurry challenge the mizzen's stiffness.

At times, the piano tinklings waft from the lounge: pure, guileless.
The navigator ponders the course, scratching behind his ear.
And the blueness of space straight ahead blends inside the spyglass
with the blueness of space withering at the rear.

II

You can tell a passenger from a sailor
by the swishing silk of his underwear,
by the quality of what he eats and where,
by the repetition of some meaningless question and a general air
of failure.

You can tell a sailor from a lieutenant
by the absence of an epaulette,
by the age that he's at,
by the nerves wrung tight like cables, or, say, a pennant.

You can tell a lieutenant from a captain
by the stripes, his hazel eyes' razzmatazz,
by the snapshot of Blanche or of Françoise,
by his reading of Kant, Maupassant, Karl Marx, and his buying
smokes by the carton.

You can tell a captain from the Admiralty
by the lonely thinking, by the profound disgust

toward anything that is blue and vast,
by the memory of his in-laws, which loses, he thinks, its accuracy.

And only a ship acts always as though she could
be another ship. Combing the waves that hold her,
a ship resembles at once an albatross and an alder
from under whose feet the ground has slipped for good.

III
Exchanges in the Lounge
"Of course the Archduke is a monster! And of course it matters!
But he's trying his best, whereas his subjects, they . . ."
"Masters resent their slaves, slaves resent their masters.
Feels like a vicious circle!" "Like a sort of ring buoy, I'd say."

"What a splendid sherry!" "Gosh, you know, I couldn't sleep a wink.
It's this frightful sun: it burns your skin through the bodice."
". . . but what if we've sprung a leak!? I've read leaks are hard
                                                        to notice.
Imagine, we've sprung a leak! And we are—to sink!

Has this ever happened to you, Lieutenant?" "No, but I have had
                                                        a sour
experience with a shark." "Yeah? But I mean, a leak. What if . . ."
"Well, then you'll finally meet the passenger from 8–F."
"Who is that?" "She's the governor's daughter, sailing to Curaçao."

IV
Exchanges on the Deck
"I, Professor, too, as a kid, wanted, and badly so,
to discover some insect, or, better still, a virus . . ."
"Right. And what happened?" "Well, science involves new values . . .
Plus, the usual tsuris . . ." "Sorry?" "You know: the dough."

"What is man, anyway? I tell you: he is a gnat!"
"But back there, in Russia, monsieur, do you also have rubber,
                                                        as in . . ."
"Valdemar! I said stop it! You bit my lip, you rat.
Don't forget, Valdemar, that I am . . ." "I am sorry, cousin."

"Listen, buddy." "Well, what?" "What is that thing far off?"
"Where?" "On the right." "I see nothing." "At two o'clock,

out there."

"Oh, that . . . maybe a whale. Got any smokes?" "Nope. Zero . . .
but—it's rising! It's rising so fast! And it is, by Jove . . ."

V

The sea is more various than the terra
firma. It's harder for you to grapple
with, not to mention stare at.
A fish is more intricate than an apple.

The land means four solid walls, a ceiling.
We are scared of wolves or of bears. Although some are ready
to detect in the latter a human feeling
and address one as "Teddy."

The sea has no room for these sorts of worries.
A whale, in its primordial splendor,
won't respond to a name like Boris;
Dick is a better tender.

The sea is filled with surprises; some are unpleasant.
Many a maritime upheaval
can't be ascribed to the evil crescent
of the moon or the human eye's lesser evil.

Ah, sea dwellers' blood is colder than ours. Their goggle
mesmerizes even fishmongers. The late Charles Darwin
would have quit legislating his gentle jungle
had he tried some limited scuba diving.

VI

Exchange on the Bridge

"Captain! We're passing the fathoms where *The Black Prince*
went down. For reasons unknown." "Navigator Benz!
Return to your cabin and sober up!"
". . . the fathoms where the Russian *Tsarina*, too, took the rap
and was lost . . ." "Navigator Benz! I'll banish you to the can!
Do you hear me?!" ". . . for reasons un . . ."

4 0

The clipper's unswerving on its blue track.
Africa, Asia, the New and the Old World lag
behind. Taut sails look like question marks in profile.
Space's answer is in the back.

Exchange in a Cabin
"Irina!" "Ah, what?" "Take a look at that thing, Irina."
"But I am asleep." "All the same. Look!" "Where?" "In the porthole.
What is that?" "Looks like somebo . . . like samba . . .

                                    like submarine . . .
                                                        Huh?
What did you say?" "But it coils!" "So what. In the water, all
things coil." "Irina!" "What? Where are you dragging me? I am
                                    completely naked."
"Yes, but just look!" "Oh, stop pushing me!" "You see?" "Well, I
look. Yes, it coils. But I think—I take it—
But it's a gigantic octopus! And it's climbing in! Nikolai!!!"

                            VIII
            The sea is ostensibly lifeless, yet
      it's full of monstrous life-forms which your mind-set
      won't grasp until you hit the king-size sea-bed.

      At times, this gets proven by what's been angled
      or by shimmering waves whose rather languid
      mirror reflects things happening under the blanket.

While on the surface, a man wants to sail fast and be there first.
            Submerged, he gets this wish reversed;
                  suddenly he feels a thirst.

            There, underneath, man feels dry within.
            Life appears to him short and green.
            Submerged, man can be only a submarine.

            From the mouth, bubbles are bursting free.
      In the eyes, an equivalent of sunrise replaces glee.
In the ears, a colorless baritone keeps uttering: "One. Two. Three."

                            4 1

"Dear Blanche, I write this to you sitting inside a gigantic octopus.
A miracle, but the stationery and your picture survived. This jelly
is hard to inhale. Yet in a sense it's populous:
there are a couple of savages, both playing the ukulele.
Main thing: it's dark. I strain my eyes and listen.
Sometimes I make out some arches and vaults. When I write, it also
                                                  becomes less black.
I resolve to examine the metabolic system.
That's the only railroad to freedom. Kisses. Your faithful Jacques."

"It's like being back in the womb . . . Still, one should be grateful
for the octopus. Sharks are worse. So is water as such—for
                                                      yours truly.
Am still searching. The savages brought a grapefruit.
But when I ask for directions, all I hear is 'Hoolie-hoolie.'
All I see are infinite, slippery, coiling tunnels.
Some peculiar, tangled system that's hard to memo-
rize. And unless I'm delirious, yesterday in these trammels
I bumped into somebody who calls himself Captain Nemo."

"Nemo again. Invited me to his rooms. I went.
He says he has reared this octopus as a protest
against society. Well, earlier, I understand,
he was married, with kids. But his wife—the hottest
pants in town . . . and so forth. And he had no choice. He says
the world drowns in Evil. The octopus ('opus' for some) avenges
hubris and heartlessness, alias earthly ways.
Promised me immortality if I don't leave the trenches."

"Tuesday. Supper at Nemo's. Caviar, cognac, *fromage*—from, I
guess, both *Prince* and *Tsarina*. The savages served: good manners.
We discussed the matter raised yesterday, that is, my
immortality; Pascal's *Pensées*; recent La Scala tenors.
Just think: evening, candles. The octopus all around.
Nemo with his goatee and baby-blue, nay, prenatal
eyes. If I think of his loneliness, my heart starts to pound . . ."

That's the last Mlle Blanche Delarue heard from Jacques Benz,
                                                      navigator.

When the ship doesn't arrive at the port of call
on time, or later on, the Business
Manager says in his office, "Hell!"
The Admiralty says, "Jesus."

Both are quite wrong. But how could they know what had
transpired? You can't interrogate a seagull
or a shark with its streamlined head.
Nor is sending an eager

doggie down the track of much help. And anyway, what sort
of tracks are there at sea? All this is valiant
bunk. One more triumph—via the absurd—
for waves contesting dry land.

Oceanic events are, as a rule, abrupt.
Still, long afterward, the waves toss the remnants of their brief sally:
life vests, splinters of masts, a rat—
none with fingerprints, sadly.

And then comes autumn. And later on, winter cuts
in. The sirocco tatters awnings that summer fancied.
Silent waves can drive the best attorney nuts
with their show of a sunset.

And what gets crystal-clear is that it's dumb to grill
(turning your vocal cords into a shortwave's risen
pitch) the blue ripples perfecting their sharp-as-steel
line of the horizon.

Something bobs up in the papers, burying under their slants
the facts, driblets really. Who can crack it . . .
A woman wearing brown clutches the drapes and slumps
slowly onto the carpet.

The horizon's improving. The air's filled with iodine and salt.
Far away, breakers pummel with great abandon
some inanimate object. And the bell of old
keeps tolling grimly at Lloyd's of London.

[*1977 / Translated by the author*]

Lines on the Winter Campaign, 1980

> *The scorching noon,*
> *the vale in Dagestan . . .*
>
> MIKHAIL LERMONTOV

I

A bullet's velocity in low temperatures
greatly depends on its target's virtues,
on its urge to warm up in the plaited muscles
of the torso, in the neck's webbed sinews.
Stones lie flat like a second army.
The shade hugs the loam to itself willy-nilly.
The sky resembles peeling stucco.
An aircraft dissolves in it like a clothes moth,
and like a spring from a ripped-up mattress
an explosion sprouts up. Outside the crater,
the blood, like boiled milk, powerless to seep into
the ground, is seized by a film's hard ripples.

II

Shepherd and sower, the North is driving
herds to the sea, spreading cold to the South.
A bright, frosty noon in a Wogistan valley.
A mechanical elephant, trunk wildly waving
at the horrid sight of the small black rodent
of a snow-covered mine, spews out throat-clogging
lumps, possessed of that old desire
of Mahomet's, to move a mountain.
Summits loom white; the celestial warehouse
lends them at noontime its flaking surplus.
The mountains lack any motion, passing
their immobility to the scattered bodies.

III

The doleful, echoing Slavic singing
at evening in Asia. Dank and freezing,
sprawling piles of human pig meat
cover the caravansary's mud bottom.
The fuel dung smolders, legs stiffen in numbness.

It smells of old socks, of forgotten bath days.
The dreams are identical, as are the greatcoats.
Plenty of cartridges, few recollections,
and the tang in the mouth of too many "hurrahs."
Glory to those who, their glances lowered,
marched in the sixties to abortion tables,
sparing the homeland its present stigma.

IV

What is contained in the drone's dull buzzing?
And what in the sound of the aero-engine?
Living is getting as complicated
as building a house with grapes' green marbles
or little lean-tos with spades and diamonds.
Nothing is stable (one puff and it's over):
families, private thoughts, clay shanties.
Night over ruins of a mountain village.
Armor, wetting its metal sheets with oil slick,
freezes in thorn scrub. Afraid of drowning
in a discarded jackboot, the moon
hides in a cloud as in Allah's turban.

V

Idle, inhaled now by no one, air.
Imported, carelessly piled-up silence.
Rising like dough that's leavened,
emptiness. If the stars had life-forms,
space would erupt with a brisk ovation;
a gunner, blinking, runs to the footlights.
Murder's a blatant way of dying,
a tautology, the art form of parrots,
a manual matter, the knack for catching
life's fly in the hairs of the gunsight
by youngsters acquainted with blood through either
hearsay or violating virgins.

VI

Pull up the blanket, dig a hole in the palliasse.
Flop down and give ear to the *oo* of the siren.
The Ice Age is coming—slavery's ice age is coming,

oozing over the atlas. Its moraines force under
nations, fond memories, muslin blouses.
Muttering, rolling our eyeballs upward,
we are becoming a new kind of bivalve,
our voice goes unheard, as though we were trilobites.
There's a draft from the corridor, draft from the square windows.
Turn off the light, wrap up in a bundle.
The vertebra craves eternity. Unlike a ringlet.
In the morning the limbs are past all uncoiling.

VII

Up in the stratosphere, thought of by no one,
the little bitch barks as she peers through the porthole:
"Beach Ball! Beach Ball! Over. It's Rover."
The beach ball's below. With the equator on it
like a dog collar. Slopes, fields, and gullies
repeat in their whiteness cheekbones
(the color of shame has all gone to the banners).
And the hens in their snowed-in hen coops,
also a-shake from the shock of reveille,
lay their eggs of immaculate color.
If anything blackens, it's just the letters,
like the tracks of some rabbit, preserved by a wonder.

[*1980 / Translated by Alan Myers*]

4 6

Café Trieste: San Francisco

To L.G.

To this corner of Grant and Vallejo
I've returned like an echo
to the lips that preferred
then a kiss to a word.

Nothing has changed here. Neither
the furniture nor the weather.
Things, in one's absence, gain
permanence, stain by stain.

Cold, through the large steamed windows
I watch the gesturing weirdos,
the bloated breams that warm
up their aquarium.

Evolving backward, a river
becomes a tear, the real
becomes memory which
can, like fingertips, pinch

just the tail of a lizard
vanishing in the desert
which was eager to fix
a traveler with a sphinx.

Your golden mane! Your riddle!
The lilac skirt, the brittle
ankles! The perfect ear
rendering "read" as "dear."

Under what cloud's pallor
now throbs the tricolor
of your future, your past
and present, swaying the mast?

Upon what linen waters
do you drift bravely toward
new shores, clutching your beads
to meet the savage needs?

Still, if sins are forgiven,
that is, if souls break even
with flesh elsewhere, this joint,
too, must be enjoyed

as afterlife's sweet parlor
where, in the clouded squalor,
saints and the ain'ts take five,
where I was first to arrive.

[*1980*]

The Hawk's Cry in Autumn

Wind from the northwestern quarter is lifting him high above
the dove-gray, crimson, umber, brown
Connecticut Valley. Far beneath,
chickens daintily pause and move
unseen in the yard of the tumbledown
farmstead, chipmunks blend with the heath.

Now adrift on the airflow, unfurled, alone,
all that he glimpses—the hills' lofty, ragged
ridges, the silver stream that threads
quivering like a living bone
of steel, badly notched with rapids,
the townships like strings of beads

strewn across New England. Having slid down to nil
thermometers—those household gods in niches—
freeze, inhibiting thus the fire
of leaves and churches' spires. Still,
no churches for him. In the windy reaches,
undreamt of by the most righteous choir,

he soars in a cobalt-blue ocean, his beak clamped shut,
his talons clutched tight into his belly
—claws balled up like a sunken fist—
sensing in each wisp of down the thrust
from below, glinting back the berry
of his eyeball, heading south-southeast

to the Rio Grande, the Delta, the beech groves and farther still:
to a nest hidden in the mighty groundswell
of grass whose edges no fingers trust,
sunk amid forest's odors, filled
with splinters of red-speckled eggshell,
with a brother or a sister's ghost.

The heart overgrown with flesh, down, feather, wing,
pulsing at feverish rate, nonstopping,

propelled by internal heat and sense,
the bird goes slashing and scissoring
the autumnal blue, yet by the same swift token,
enlarging it at the expense

of its brownish speck, barely registering on the eye,
a dot, sliding far above the lofty
pine tree; at the expense of the empty look
of that child, arching up at the sky,
that couple that left the car and lifted
their heads, that woman on the stoop.

But the uprush of air is still lifting him
higher and higher. His belly feathers
feel the nibbling cold. Casting a downward gaze,
he sees the horizon growing dim,
he sees, as it were, the features
of the first thirteen colonies whose

chimneys all puff out smoke. Yet it's their total within his sight
that tells the bird of his elevation,
of what altitude he's reached this trip.
What am I doing at such a height?
He senses a mixture of trepidation
and pride. Heeling over a tip

of wing, he plummets down. But the resilient air
bounces him back, winging up to glory,
to the colorless icy plane.
His yellow pupil darts a sudden glare
of rage, that is, a mix of fury
and terror. So once again

he turns and plunges down. But as walls return
rubber balls, as sins send a sinner to faith, or near,
he's driven upward this time as well!
He! whose innards are still so warm!
Still higher! Into some blasted ionosphere!
That astronomically objective hell

of birds that lacks oxygen, and where the milling stars
play millet served from a plate or a crescent.
What, for the bipeds, has always meant
height, for the feathered is the reverse.
Not with his puny brain but with shriveled air sacs
he guesses the truth of it: it's the end.

And at this point he screams. From the hooklike beak
there tears free of him and flies *ad luminem*
the sound Erinyes make to rend
souls: a mechanical, intolerable shriek,
the shriek of steel that devours aluminum;
"mechanical," for it's meant

for nobody, for no living ears:
not man's, not yelping foxes',
not squirrels' hurrying to the ground
from branches; not for tiny field mice whose tears
can't be avenged this way, which forces
them into their burrows. And only hounds

lift up their muzzles. A piercing, high-pitched squeal,
more nightmarish than the D-sharp grinding
of the diamond cutting glass,
slashes the whole sky across. And the world seems to reel
for an instant, shuddering from this rending.
For the warmth burns space in the highest as

badly as some iron fence down here
brands incautious gloveless fingers.
We, standing where we are, exclaim
"There!" and see far above the tear
that is a hawk, and hear the sound that lingers
in wavelets, a spider skein

swelling notes in ripples across the blue vault of space
whose lack of echo spells, especially in October,
an apotheosis of pure sound.
And caught in this heavenly patterned lace,

starlike, spangled with hoarfrost powder,
silver-clad, crystal-bound,

the bird sails to the zenith, to the dark-blue high
of azure. Through binoculars we foretoken
him, a glittering dot, a pearl.
We hear something ring out in the sky,
like some family crockery being broken,
slowly falling aswirl,

yet its shards, as they reach our palms, don't hurt
but melt when handled. And in a twinkling
once more one makes out curls, eyelets, strings,
rainbowlike, multicolored, blurred
commas, ellipses, spirals, linking
heads of barley, concentric rings—

the bright doodling pattern the feather once possessed,
a map, now a mere heap of flying
pale flakes that make a green slope appear
white. And the children, laughing and brightly dressed,
swarm out of doors to catch them, crying
with a loud shout in English, "Winter's here!"

[*1975* / *Translated by Alan Myers and the author*]

Sextet

To Mark Strand

I

An eyelid is twitching. From the open mouth
gushes silence. The cities of Europe mount
each other at railroad stations. A pleasant odor
of soap tells the jungle dweller of the approaching foe.
Wherever you set your sole or toe,
the world map develops blank spots, grows balder.

A palate goes dry. The traveler's seized by thirst.
Children, to whom the worst
should be done, fill the air with their shrieks. An eyelid twitches
all the time. As for columns, from
the thick of them someone always emerges. Even in your sweet dream,
even with your eyes shut, you see human features.

And it wells up in your throat like barf:
"Give me ink and paper and, as for yourself,
scram!" And an eyelid is twitching. Odd, funereal
whinings—as though someone's praying upstairs—poison the
daily grind.
The monstrosity of what's happening in your mind
makes unfamiliar premises look familiar.

II

Sometimes in the desert you hear a voice. You fetch
a camera in order to catch the face.
But—too dark. Sit down, then, release your hearing
to the Southern lilt of a small monkey who
left her palm tree but, having no leisure to
become a human, went straight to whoring.

Better sail by steamer, horizon's ant,
taking part in geography, in blueness, and
not in history, this dry land's scabies.
Better trek across Greenland on skis and camp

among the icebergs, among the plump
walruses as they bathe their babies.

The alphabet won't allow your trip's goal to be
ever forgotten, that famed point B.
There a crow caws hard, trying to play the raven;
there a black sheep bleats, rye is choked with weeds;
there the top brass, like furriers, shear out bits
of the map's faded pelt, so that they look even.

III

For thirty-six years I've stared at fire.
An eyelid is twitching. Both palms perspire:
the cop leaves the room with your papers. Angst. Built to calm it,
an obelisk, against its will, recedes
in a cloud, amidst bright seeds,
like an immobile comet.

Night. With your hair quite gone, you still dine alone,
being your own grand master, your own black pawn.
The kipper's soiling a headline about striking rickshaws
or a berserk volcano's burps—
God knows where, in other words—
flitting its tail over "The New Restrictions."

I comprehend only the buzz of flies
in the Eastern bazaars! On the sidewalk, flat
on his back, the traveler strains his sinews,
catching the air with his busted gills.
In the afterlife, the pain that kills
here no doubt continues.

IV

"Where's that?" asks the nephew, toying with his stray locks.
And, fingering brown mountain folds, "Here," pokes
the niece. In the depths of the garden, yellow
swings creak softly. The table dwarfs a bouquet
of violets. The sun's splattering the parquet
floor. From the drawing room float twangs of a cello.

At night, a plateau absorbs moonshine.
A boulder shepherds its elephantine
shadow. A brook's silver change is spending
itself in a gully. Clutched sheets in a room elude
their milky/swarthy/abandoned nude—
an anonymous painful painting.

In spring, labor ants build their muddy coops;
rooks show up; so do creatures with other groups
of blood; a fresh leaf shelters
the verging shame of two branches. In autumn, a sky hawk keeps
counting villages' chicklets; and the sahib's
white jacket is dangling from the servant's shoulders.

                              v

Was the word ever uttered? And then—if yes—
in what language? And where? And how much ice
should be thrown into a glass to halt a *Titanic*
of thought? Does the whole recall the neat shapes of parts?
Would a botanist, suddenly facing birds
in an aquarium, panic?

Now let us imagine an absolute emptiness.
A place without time. The air *per se*. In this,
in that, and in the third direction—pure, simple, pallid
air. A Mecca of it: oxygen, nitrogen. In which
there's really nothing except for the rapid twitch-
ing of a lonely eyelid.

These are the notes of a naturalist. The naughts
on nature's own list. Stained with flowerpots.
A tear falls in a vacuum without acceleration.
The last of hotbed neu-roses, hearing the
faint buzzing of time's tsetse,
I smell increasingly of isolation.

                             VI

And I dread my petals' joining the crowned knot
of fire! Most resolutely not!

                            5 5

Oh, but to know the place for the first, the second,
and the umpteenth time! When everything comes to light,
when you hear or utter the jewels like
"When I was in the army" or "Change the record!"

Petulant is the soul begging mercy from
an invisible or dilated frame.
Still, if it comes to the point where the blue acrylic
dappled with cirrus suggests the Lord,
say, "Give me strength to sustain the hurt,"
and learn it by heart like a decent lyric.

When you are no more, unlike the rest,
the latter may think of themselves as blessed
with the place so much safer thanks to the big withdrawal
of what your conscience indeed amassed.
And a fish that prophetically shines with rust
will splash in a pond and repeat your oval.

[1976 / Translated by the author]

Minefield Revisited

You, guitar-shaped affair with tousled squalor
of chords, who keep looming brown in an empty parlor,
or snow-white against laundered expanses, or
dark—at dusk especially—in the corridor,
strum me a tune of how drapery makes its cloudy
rustle, how a flipped-up switch ravages half a body
with shadow, how a fly prowls the atlas, how in the garden
outside, the sunset echoes a steaming squadron
of which there survived only a middy blouse
in the nursery, how hidden in the satin trousers
the comb of a Turkish dog trainer, when played, elevates his poodle
beyond Kovalevska, beyond its idol
to a happy occasion: that is, to yelping forty
times at some birthday, while wet and frothy
firework stars fizz and fade in the foggy trembling
glass, and carafes on a tablecloth feign the Kremlin.

[*1978 / Translated by the author*]

Near Alexandria

To Carl Proffer

The concrete needle is shooting its
heroin into cumulous wintry muscle.
From a trash can, a spy plucks the crumpled morsel—
a blueprint of ruins—and glances east.

Ubiquitous figures on horseback: all
four hooves glued to their marble bracket.
The warriors apparently kicked the bucket,
crushing bedbugs on the linen sprawl.

In the twilight, chandeliers gleam, akin
to bonfires; sylphides weave their sweet pattern:
a finger, eight hours poised by the button
relaxes fondling its hooded twin.

Windowpanes quiver with tulle's soft ply;
the besom of naked shrubs is bothered
by the evergreen rustle of money, by the
seemingly nonstop July.

A cross between a blade and a raw
throat uttering no sound whatever,
the sharp bend of a level river
glistens, covered with icy straw.

Victim of lungs though friend to words,
the air is transparent, severely punctured
by beaks that treat it as pens treat parchment,
by visible-only-in-profile birds.

This is a flattened colossus veiled
by the gauze thickening on the horizon,
edged with the lacework of wheels gone frozen
after six by the curb's gray welt.

Like the mouse creeping out of the scarlet crack,
the sunset gnaws hungrily the electric
cheese of the outskirts, erected
by those who clearly trust their knack

for surviving everything: by termites.
Warehouses, surgeries. Having measured
there the proximity of the desert,
the cinnamon-tinted earth waylays its

horizontality in the fake
pyramids, porticoes, rooftops' ripple,

as the train creeps knowingly, like a snake,
to the capital's only nipple.

[*1982 / Translated by the author*]

Tsushima Screen

The perilous yellow sun follows with its slant eyes
masts of the shuddered grove steaming up to capsize
in the frozen straits of Epiphany. February has fewer
days than the other months; therefore, it's more cruel
than the rest. Dearest, it's more sound
to wrap up our sailing round
the globe with habitual naval grace,
moving your cot to the fireplace
where our dreadnought is going under
in great smoke. Only fire can grasp a winter!
Golden unharnessed stallions in the chimney
dye their manes to more corvine shades as they near the finish,
and the dark room fills with the plaintive, incessant chirring
of a naked, lounging grasshopper one cannot cup in fingers.

[*1978* / *Translated by the author*]

A Martial Law Carol

To Wiktor Woroszylski and Andrzej Drawicz

One more Christmas ends
soaking stripes and stars.
All my Polish friends
are behind steel bars,
locked like zeroes in
some graph sheet of wrath:
as a discipline
slavery beats math.

Nations learn the rules
like a naughty boy
as the tyrant drools
manacles in joy.
One pen stroke apiece,
minus edits plus
helping the police
to subtract a class.

From a stubborn brow
something scarlet drops
on the Christmas snow.
As it turns, the globe's
face gets uglier,
pores becoming cells,
while the planets glare
coldly, like ourselves.

Hungry faces. Grime.
Squalor. Unabashed
courts distribute time
to the people crushed
not so much by tanks
or by submachine
guns as by the banks
we deposit in.

Deeper than the depth
of your thoughts or mine
is the sleep of death
in the Vujek mine;
higher than your rent
is that hand whose craft
keeps the others bent—
as though photographed.

Powerless is speech.
Still, it bests a tear
in attempts to reach,
crossing the frontier,
for the heavy hearts
of my Polish friends.
One more trial starts.
One more Christmas ends.

[*1980*]

Folk Tune

It's not that the Muse feels like clamming up,
it's more like high time for the lad's last nap.
And the scarf-waving lass who wished him the best
drives a steamroller across his chest.

And the words won't rise either like that rod
or like logs to rejoin their old grove's sweet rot,
and, like eggs in the frying pan, the face
spills its eyes all over the pillowcase.

Are you warm tonight under those six veils
in that basin of yours whose strung bottom wails;
where like fish that gasp at the foreign blue
my raw lip was catching what then meant you?

I would have hare's ears sewn to my bald head,
in thick woods for your sake I'd gulp drops of lead,
and from black gnarled snags in the oil-smooth pond
I'd bob up to your face as some *Tirpitz* won't.

But it's not on the cards or the waiter's tray,
and it pains to say where one's hair turns gray.
There are more blue veins than the blood to swell
their dried web, let alone some remote brain cell.

We are parting for good, little friend, that's that.
Draw an empty circle on your yellow pad.
This will be me: no insides in thrall.
Stare at it a while, then erase the scrawl.

[*1980 / Translated by the author*]

Roman Elegies

To Benedetta Craveri

I

The captive mahogany of a private Roman
flat. In the ceiling, a dust-covered crystal island.
At sunset, the windowpanes pan a common
ground for the nebulous and the ironed.
Setting a naked foot on the rosy marble,
the body steps toward its future: to its attire.
If somebody shouted "Freeze!" I'd perform that marvel
as this city happily did in its childhood hour.
The world's made of nakedness and of foldings.
Still, the latter's richer with love than a face, that's certain.
Thus an opera tenor's so sweet to follow
since he yields invariably to a curtain.
By nightfall, a blue eye employs a tear,
cleansing, to a needless shine, the iris;
and the moon overhead apes an emptied square
with no fountain in it. But of rock as porous.

II

The month of stalled pendulums. Only a fly in August
in a dry carafe's throat is droning its busy hymn.
The numerals on the clock face crisscross like earnest
anti-aircraft searchlights probing for seraphim.
The month of drawn blinds, of furniture wrapped in cotton
shrouds, of the sweating double in the mirror above the cupboard,
of bees that forget the topography of their hives and, coated
with suntan honey, keep staggering seaward.
Get busy then, faucet, over the snow-white, sagging
muscle, tousle the tufts of thin gray singes!
To a homeless torso and its idle, grabby
mitts, there's nothing as dear as the sight of ruins.
And they, in their turn, see themselves in the broken Jewish
r no less gladly: for the pieces fallen
so apart, saliva's the only solution they wish
for, as time's barbarous corneas scan the Forum.

The tiled, iron-hot, glowing hills: midsummer.
Clouds feel like angels, thanks to their cooling shadows.
Thus the bold cobblestone eyes, like a happy sinner,
the blue underthings of your leggy blond friend. A bard of
trash, extra thoughts, broken lines, unmanly,
I hide in the bowels of the Eternal City
from the luminary that rolled back so many
marble pupils with rays bright enough for setting
up yet another universe. A yellow square. Noontime's
stupor. A Vespa's owner tortures the screaming gears.
Clutching my chest with my hand, at a distance
I reckon the change from the well-spent years.
And, like a book at once opened to all its pages,
the laurels scratch the scorched white of a balustrade.
And the Colosseum looms, the skull of Argus,
through whose sockets clouds drift like a thought of the vanished herd.

Two young brunettes in the library of the husband
of the more stunning one. Two youthful, tender
ovals hunch over pages: a Muse telling Fate the substance
of several things she tried to render.
The swish of old paper, of red crepe de Chine. A humming
fan mixes violets, lavender, and carnations.
Braiding of hair: an elbow thrusts up its summit
accustomed to cumulus-thick formations.
Oh, a dark eye is obviously more fluent
in brown furniture, pomegranates, oak shutters.
It's more keen, it's more cordial than a blue one;
to the blue one, though, nothing matters!
The blue one can always tell the owner
from the goods, especially before closing—
that is, time from living—and turn the latter over,
as tails strain to look at heads in tossing.

Jig, little candle tongue, over the empty paper,
bow to the rotten breath as though you were courted,

follow—but don't get too close!—the pauper
letters standing in line to obtain the content.
You animate the walls, wardrobe, the sill's sweetbriar:
more than handwriting is ever after;
even your soot, it appears, soars higher
than the holiest wish of these musings' author.
Still, in their midst you earn yourself a decent
name, as my fountain pen, in memory of your tender
commas, in Rome, at the millennium's end, produces
a lantern, a cresset, a torch, a taper,
never a period—and the premises look their ancient
selves, from the severed head down to a yellow toenail.
For an ink pot glows bright whenever someone mentions
light, especially in a tunnel.

VI

Clicking of a piano at the siesta hour.
Stillness of sleepy mews acquires
C-flats, as scales coat a fish which narrows
round the corner. Exhaling quarrels,
inhaling a fusty noon's air, the stucco
flaps its brown gills, and a sultry, porous
cavity of a mouth scatters
around cold pearls of Horace.
I've never built that cloud-thrusting stony
object that could explain clouds' pallor.
I've learned about my own, and any
fate, from a letter, from its black color.
Thus some fall asleep while hugging
a Leica, in order to take a picture
of the dream, to make themselves out, having
awakened in a developed future.

VII

Eggshells of cupolas, vertebrae of bell towers.
Colonnades' limbs sprawled wide in their blissful, heathen
leisure. The square root of a skylark scours
the bottomless, as though prior to prayers, heaven.
Light reaps much more than it has sown: an awkward

body hides in a crack while its shadow shutters
walls. In these parts, all windows are looking northward,
where the more one boozes the less one matters.
North! A white iceberg's frozen-in piano;
smallpoxed with quartz, vases' granite figures;
a plain unable to stop field-glass scanning;
sweet Ashkenazy's ten running fingers.
Never again are the legions to thread those contours:
to a creaking pen, even its words won't hearken.
And the golden eyebrow—as, at sunset, a cornice—
rises up, and the eyes of the darling darken.

VIII

In these squinting alleyways, where even a thought about
one's self is too cumbersome, in this furrowed clutter
of the brain which has long since refused to cloud
the universe, where now keyed up, now scattered,
you trundle your boots on the cobbled, checkered
squares, from a fountain and back to a Caesar—
thus a needle shuffles across the record
skipping its grooves—it is altogether
proper to settle now for a measly fraction
of remaining life, for the past life craving
completeness, for its attempts to fashion
an integer. The sound the heels are scraping
from the ground is the aria of their union,
a serenade that what-has-been-longer
hums to what's-to-be-shorter. This is a genuine
Caruso for a gramophone-dodging mongrel.

IX

Lesbia, Julia, Cynthia, Livia, Michelina.
Bosoms, ringlets of fleece: for effects, and for causes also.
Heaven-baked clay, fingertips' brave arena.
Flesh that renders eternity an anonymous torso.
You breed immortals: those who have seen you bare,
they too turned Catulluses, statues, heavy
Neros, et cetera. Short-term goddesses! you are
much more a joy to believe in than a permanent bevy.

Hail the smooth abdomen, thighs as their hamstrings tighten.
White upon white, as Kazimir's dream image
one summer evening, I, the most mortal item
in the midst of this wreckage resembling the whole world's rib cage,
sip with feverish lips wine from a tender collar-
bone; the sky is as pale as a cheek with a mole that trembles;
and the cupolas bulge like the tits of the she-wolf, fallen
asleep after having fed her Romulus and her Remus.

X

Mimicking local pines, embrace the ether!
The fingertips won't cull much more than the pane's tulle quiver.
Still, a little black bird won't return from the sky blue, either.
And we, too, aren't gods in miniature, that's clear.
That's precisely why we are happy: because we are nothings; speckled
pores are spurned by summits or sharp horizons;
the body is space's reversal, no matter how hard you pedal.
And when we are unhappy, it's perhaps for the same small reasons.
Better lean on a portico, loose the white shirt that billows,
stone cools the spinal column, gray pigeons mutter,
and watch how the sun is sinking into gardens and distant villas,
how the water—the tutor
of eloquence—pours from the rusted lips, repeating
not a thing, save a nymph with her marble truants,
save that it's cold and fresh, save that it's splitting
the face into rippling ruins.

XI

Private life. Fears, shredded thoughts, the jagged
blanket renders the contours of Europe meager.
By means of a blue shirt and a rumpled jacket
something still gets reflected in the wardrobe mirror.
Let's have some tea, face, so that the teeth may winnow
lips. Yoked by a ceiling, the air grows flatter.
Cast inadvertently through the window,
a glance makes a bunch of blue jays flutter
from their pine tops. A room in Rome, white paper,
the tail of a freshly drawn letter: a darting rodent.

Thus, thanks to the perfect perspective, some objects peter
out; thus, still others shuffle across the frozen
Tanaïs, dropping from the picture, limping,
occiputs covered with wilted laurels and blizzards' powder—
toward Time, lying beyond the limits
of every spraddling superpower.

XII

Lean over. I'll whisper something to you: I am
grateful for everything: for the chicken cartilage
and for the chirr of scissors already cutting
out the void for me—for it is your hem.
Doesn't matter if it's pitch-black, doesn't matter if
it holds nothing: no ovals, no limbs to count.
The more invisible something is,
the more certain it's been around,
and the more obviously it's everywhere. You
were the first to whom all this happened, were you?
For a nail holding something one would divide by two—
were it not for remainders—there is no gentler quarry.
I was in Rome. I was flooded by light. The way
a splinter can only dream about.
Golden coins on the retina are to stay—
enough to last one through the whole blackout.

[1981 / Translated by the author]

To Urania

To I.K.

Everything has its limit, including sorrow.
A windowpane stalls a stare. Nor does a grill abandon
a leaf. One may rattle the keys, gurgle down a swallow.
Loneliness cubes a man at random.
A camel sniffs at the rail with a resentful nostril;
a perspective cuts emptiness deep and even.
And what is space anyway if not the
body's absence at every given
point? That's why Urania's older than sister Clio!
In daylight or with the soot-rich lantern,
you see the globe's pate free of any bio,
you see she hides nothing, unlike the latter.
There they are, blueberry-laden forests,
rivers where the folk with bare hands catch sturgeon
or the towns in whose soggy phone books
you are starring no longer; farther eastward surge on
brown mountain ranges; wild mares carousing
in tall sedge; the cheekbones get yellower
as they turn numerous. And still farther east, steam dreadnoughts
or cruisers,

and the expanse grows blue like lace underwear.

[1981 / Translated by the author]

The Bust of Tiberius

All hail to you, two thousand years too late.
I, too, once took a whore in marriage.
We have some things in common. Plus,
all round, your city. Bustle, shrieking traffic.
Damp alleyways with hypodermic youths.
Also, the ruins. I, a standard stranger,
salute your grimy bust in some
dank chamber storing echoes. Ah, Tiberius!
Here you're not thirty yet. The face displays
a greater confidence in trusted sinews
than in the future of their sum. A head
the sculptor severs in one's lifetime surely
sounds like a prophecy of power. All
that lies below the massive jawbone—Rome:
the provinces, the latifundists, the cohorts,
plus swarms of infants bubbling at your ripe
stiff sausage. A delight in tune
with nourishment by the she-wolf of tiny
Remus and Romulus—the mouths of babes indeed!
that sweetly incoherent mumbling
inside the toga! So we have a bust
that stands for the essential independence
of brain from body: (a) one's own, (b) one
that is Imperial. Should you be carving your
own likeness, you'd produce gray twisted matter.

You haven't reached thirty yet, thus far. Not one
arresting feature to detain observers.
Nor, in its turn, does your observant eye
appear to rest on anything before it:
neither on someone's face nor on
some classic landscape. Ah, Tiberius!
What does it matter what Suetonius
cum Tacitus still mutter, seeking causes
for your great cruelty? There are no causes in
this world—effects alone. And people
are victims of their own effects,

the more so in those steamy dungeons
where everyone confesses. Though confessions
dragged out by torture, like the ones in childhood,
are of a muchness. Far the best of fates
is really to have no part of truth.
It never elevates us. None,
Caesars especially. And at any rate
you seem a man more capable of drowning
in your piscina than in some deep thought.
Plus, shouldn't cruelty be termed a form
of speeding matters up, accelerating
the common fate of things? of a simple body's
free fall in vacuum?—in which, alas,
one always finds oneself when one is falling.

New year. A January pile of clouds
above the wintry town, like extra marble.
The brown, reality-escaping Tiber
and fountains spouting up to where no one
peers down—through lowered eyelids or
through fingers splayed. Another era!
And no one's up to holding by the ears
the wolves consumed with frenzy. Ah, Tiberius!
And such as we presume to judge you? You
were surely a monster, though perhaps more monstrous
was your indifference. But isn't it monsters
—not victims, no—that nature generates
in her own likeness? Ah, how much more soothing
(that is to say, if one should get the choice)
to be wiped off the earth by hell-bound fiends
than by neurotics. Still in your twenties,
with stony looks hewn out of stone, you look
a durable organic engine
of pure annihilation: not some dope,
a slave of passion, channel of ideas,
et cetera. And to defend you from
harsh tongues is like defending oak trees
from leaves, wrapped in their meaningless but clearly
insistent clamor of majority.

An empty gallery. A murky noontime
soiling tall windows with the distant drone
of life. A piece of marble in no fashion
responding to the quality of space . . .
It cannot be that you don't hear me speaking!
I, too, have often made that headlong dash
from rank reality. I, too, became an island
replete with ruins, ostriches. I, too,
struck off a profile with the aid of lamplight.
As for the things I've either coined or said,
it must be said that what I've said is useless,
and not eventually, but already: now.
Can't that be also that acceleration
of history? A bold attempt, alas,
by consequence to overtake causation?
And also in a total vacuum, which
gives no assurance of impressive splashdown.
Should one recant, then? rearrange the dice?
cut yet another deck of cards or atlas?
Who gives a damn: the radioactive rain
will scour us much the same as your historian.
Who'll come around to curse us, then? a star?
the moon? some wandering termite, driven
mad with its multiple mutations, fat
and yolklike? Probably. But having hit
something that's hard in us, it too, I reckon,
will shudder and give up its digging.

"Bust," it will utter in the tongue of ruins
and of contracting muscles. "Bust. Bust. Bust."

[*1981 / Translated by Alan Myers and the author*]

7 3

Seven Strophes

I was but what you'd brush
with your palm, what your leaning
brow would hunch to in evening's
raven-black hush.

I was but what your gaze
in that dark could distinguish:
a dim shape to begin with,
later—features, a face.

It was you, on my right,
on my left, with your heated
sighs, who molded my helix,
whispering at my side.

It was you by that black
window's trembling tulle pattern
who laid in my raw cavern
a voice calling you back.

I was practically blind.
You, appearing, then hiding,
gave me my sight and heightened
it. Thus some leave behind

a trace. Thus they make worlds.
Thus, having done so, at random
wastefully they abandon
their work to its whirls.

Thus, prey to speeds
of light, heat, cold, or darkness,
a sphere in space without markers
spins and spins.

[*1981   /   Translated by Paul Graves*]

The Residence

An attractive mansion on the avenue of Sardanapalus.
A pair of cast-iron lions with their hind legs complex.
In the hall, like a grinning footman, the black Steinway lets
the owner's fat-fingered, myopic, porous
grandniece poke its molars in broad daylight.
Lavender smells. Everywhere, including the kitchen,
outnumbering dishes, hang oils and etchings
depicting the Teacher, whose kinfolk might
still be living somewhere in Europe. Hence, sets of Goethe, plus
some Balzacs, chandeliers, capitals, gay putti,
and the very columns whose supple body
houses a battery of the "ground-to-ground" class.

But it feels the coziest in the eastern, i.e., his wing.
Bedroom windows hug poplars, or else it's alders.
And the cricket's chirr's softer than all those idle
bird feeders with their sensitive relay wink.
Here in the evening you may snap the lock, undress
to the lilac sweat shirt, to the matching long johns, whatever.
A far-off crow's nest in the branches suggests the beaver
of a Jewess he knew in his salad days,
but thank heaven they've split. And what really makes you crawl
to the bed are those eight-digit budget figures routinely hoarded
by the staff, or the last mortal screams of his confessed-it-all
son, apparently tape-recorded.

[*1983 / Translated by the author*]

Eclogue IV: Winter

To Derek Walcott

Ultima Cumaei venit iam carminis aetas;
magnus ab integro saeclorum nascitu ordo.
— VERGIL, *Eclogue IV*

I

In winter it darkens the moment lunch is over.
It's hard then to tell starving men from sated.
A yawn keeps a phrase from leaving its cozy lair.
The dry, instant version of light, the opal
snow, dooms tall alders—by having freighted
them—to insomnia, to your glare,

well after midnight. Forget-me-nots and roses
crop up less frequently in dialogues. Dogs with languid
fervor pick up the trail, for they, too, leave traces.
Night, having entered the city, pauses
as in a nursery, finds a baby under the blanket.
And the pen creaks like steps that are someone else's.

II

My life has dragged on. In the recitative of a blizzard
a keen ear picks up the tune of the Ice Age.
Every "Down in the Valley" is, for sure,
a chilled boogie-woogie. A bitter, brittle
cold represents, as it were, a message
to the body of its final temperature

or—the earth itself, sighing out of habit
for its galactic past, its sub-zero horrors.
Cheeks burn crimson like radishes even here.
Cosmic space is always shot through with matte agate,
and the beeping Morse, returning homeward,
finds no ham operator's ear.

III

In February, lilac retreats to osiers.
Imperative to a snowman's profile,

7 6

carrots get more expensive. Limited by a brow,
a glance at cold, metallic objects
is fiercer than the metal itself. This, while
you peel eyes from objects, still may allow

no shedding of blood. The Lord, some reckon,
was reviewing His world in this very fashion
on the eighth day and after. In winter, we're
not berry pickers: we stuff the cracks with oakum,
praise the common good with a greater passion,
and things grow older by, say, a year.

IV

In great cold, pavements glaze like a sugar candy,
steam from the mouth suggests a dragon,
if you dream of a door, you tend to slam it.
My life has dragged on. The signs are plenty.
They'd make yet another life, just as dragging.
From these signs alone one would compose a climate

or a landscape. Preferably with no people,
with virgin white through a lacework shroud,
—a world where nobody heard of Parises, Londons; where
weekdays are spun by diffusive, feeble
light; where, too, in the end you shudder
spotting the ski tracks . . . Well, just a pair.

V

Time equals cold. Each body, sooner
or later, falls prey to a telescope. With the years,
it moves away from the luminary, grows colder.
Hoarfrost jungles the windowpane with sumac,
ferns, or horsetail, with what appears
to be nursed on this glass and deprived of color

by loneliness. But, as with a marble hero,
one's eye rolls up rather than runs in winter.
Where sight fails, yielding to dreams' swarmed forces,
time, fallen sharply beneath the zero,
burns your brain like the index finger
of a scamp from popular Russian verses.

My life has dragged on. One cold resembles another
cold. Time looks like time. What sets them apart is only
a warm body. Mule-like, stubborn creature,
it stands firmly between them, rather
like a border guard: stiffened, sternly
preventing the wandering of the future

into the past. In winter, to put it bleakly,
Tuesday is Saturday. The daytime is a deceiver:
Are the lights out already? Or not yet on? It's chilly.
Dailies might as well be printed weekly.
Time stares at a looking glass like a diva
who's forgotten what's on tonight: *Tosca*? Oh no, *Lucia*?

Dreams in the frozen season are longer, keener.
The patchwork quilt and the parquet deal,
on their mutual squares, in chessboard warriors.
The hoarser the blizzard rules the chimney,
the hotter the quest for a pure ideal
of naked flesh in a cotton vortex,

and you dream nasturtiums' stubborn odor,
a tuft of cobwebs shading a corner nightly,
in a narrow ravine torrid Terek's splashes,
a feast of fingertips caught in shoulder
straps. And then all goes quiet. Idly
an ember smolders in dawn's gray ashes.

Cold values space. Baring no rattling sabers,
it takes hill and dale, townships and hamlets
(the populace cedes without trying
tricks), mostly cities, whose great ensembles,
whose arches and colonnades, in hundreds,
stand like prophets of cold's white triumph,

looming wanly. Cold is gliding
from the sky on a parachute. Each and every column

looks like a fifth, desires an overthrow.
Only the crow doesn't take snow gladly.
And you often hear the angry, solemn,
patriotic gutturals speaking crow.

IX

In February, the later it is, the lower
the mercury. More time means more cold. Stars, scattered
like a smashed thermometer, turn remotest
regions of night into a strep marvel.
In daytime, when sky is akin to stucco,
Malevich himself wouldn't have noticed

them, white on white. That's why angels
are invisible. To their legions
cold is of benefit. We would make them
out, the winged ones, had our eyes' angle
been indeed on high, where they are linking
in white camouflage like Finnish marksmen.

X

For me, other latitudes have no usage.
I am skewered by cold like a grilled-goose portion.
Glory to naked birches, to the fir-tree needle,
to the yellow bulb in an empty passage—
glory to everything set by the wind in motion:
at a ripe age, it can replace the cradle.

The North is the honest thing. For it keeps repeating
all your life the same stuff—whispering, in full volume,
in the life dragged on, in all kinds of voices;
and toes freeze numb in your deerskin creepers,
reminding you, as you complete your polar
conquest, of love, of shivering under clock faces.

XI

In great cold, distance won't sing like sirens.
In space, the deepest inhaling hardly
ensures exhaling, nor does departure
a return. Time is the flesh of the silent

7 9

cosmos. Where nothing ticks. Even being hurtled
out of the spacecraft, one wouldn't capture

any sounds on the radio—neither fox-trots nor maidens
wailing from a hometown station.
What kills you out there, in orbit, isn't
the lack of oxygen but the abundance
of time in its purest (with no addition
of your life) form. It's hard to breathe it.

XII

Winter! I cherish your bitter flavor
of cranberries, tangerine crescents on faience saucers,
the tea, sugar-frosted almonds (at best, two ounces).
You were opening our small beaks in favor
of names like Marina or Olga—morsels
of tenderness at that age that fancies

cousins. I sing a snowpile's blue contours
at dusk, rustling foil, clicking B-flat somewhere,
as though "Chopsticks" were tried by the Lord's own finger.
And the logs, which rattled in stony courtyards
of the gray, dank city that freezes bare
by the sea, are still warming my every fiber.

XIII

At a certain age, the time of year, the season
coincides with fate. Theirs is a brief affair.
But on days like this you sense you are right. Your worries
about things that haven't come your way are ceasing,
and a simple botanist may take care
of commenting upon daily life and mores.

In this period, eyes lose their green of nettles,
the triangle drops its geometric ardor:
all the angles drawn with cobwebs are fuzzy.
In exchanges on death, place matters
more and more than time. The cold gets harder.
And saliva suddenly burns its cozy

8 0

tongue, like that coin. Still, all the rivers
are ice-locked. You can put on long johns and trousers,
strap steel runners to boots with ropes and a piece of timber.
Teeth, worn out by the tap dance of shivers,
won't rattle because of fear. And the Muse's
voice gains a reticent, private timbre.

That's the birth of an eclogue. Instead of the shepherd's signal,
a lamp's flaring up. Cyrillic, while running witless
on the pad as though to escape the captor,
knows more of the future than the famous sibyl:
of how to darken against the whiteness,
as long as the whiteness lasts. And after.

[*1977 / Translated by the author*]

Eclogue V: Summer

To Margo Picken

I hear you again, mosquito hymn of summer!
In the dogwood tepee, ants sweat in slumber.
A botfly slides off the burdock's crumpled
epaulet, showing us that it always
ranked just a private. And caterpillars show us
the meaning of "lower than grass." The rosebays'

overgrown derricks—knee-deep or ankle-
deep in the couch-grass and bindweed jungle—
shine blue from their proximity and their angle
to the zenith. The praying mantis's little
rakes shutter the hemlock's brittle,
colorless fireworks. The scruffy, whittled

thistle's heart looks like a land-mine which is
only half exploding its ruddy riches.
The cowbane resembles a hand that reaches
for a carafe. And, like a fisherman's wife, a spider
patches its trawl, strung out between the bitter
wormwood and the hedge mustard's golden miter.

Life is the sum of trifling motions. The silver
twilight of sedge's sheathed blades, the quiver
of many a shepherd's purse, the ever-
shifting tableau of horse sorrel, gentle
alfalfa's ditherings—these engender
our grasp of the rules of a stage whose center

cannot be found. At noonday both wheat and shabby
darnel cast northward their common shadow
because they are sown and shuffled
by the same windy sower about whose humors
the place is still rife with all sorts of rumors.
Give ear to the swishing murmurs

of cock-and-hen brushes! To what a daisy's
odd-or-even whispers! To how a drowsy
coltsfoot dubs these findings crazy.
To how a soft, wild-mint Leda, flattened
by a powerful swanweed, goes raving mad and
mumbles. Small grassplots of summer, flooded

with sunlight! Their homeless moths! Their nettle
pyramids! Their heat! Their total
stupor! Their fern pagoda's gentle
sway, or their ruined column
of anise, or a bent minaret of wild sage's solemn
bow—that's a copy, in grass and pollen,

of Babylon! Terzaromeville's verdant recent
version! The realm where, turning left, one's risking
ending up on the right side: everything's close, yet distant!
And a grasshopper in his pursuit of beauty—
of the cabbage butterfly in her pale tutu—
stalls, a knight at the crossroads, caught in dry blades' tutti.

II

Air, that's colorless in its core, seems, given
a landscape, blue—very often even
dark blue. The green perhaps gets enlivened
in a similar fashion. A passive grimace,
an eye's remoteness from the weed's the greenness
of the weed. In July, the seamless

flora's clear penchant to sunder
its ties with a botanist while darkening sanguine
leaves results in pale faces' suntan.
The sum of beautiful ones and ugly,
coming close or retreating, oddly
enough, can waste one's eye as badly

as these green/blue expanses. The color's humble
mask hides infinity's constant hunger
for details. Mass, after all, is hardly

the result of energy split by the square
of the speed of light (nay, sight!) somewhere
but the feeling of friction, of wear and tear

against one's own likes. Examine
space closely! Its selfsame garment
nearby and far away! Its ardent
obstinacy, with which green or bluish hollows—
their distance notwithstanding—always
sustain the pigment. Ah, this is almost

faith! A fanatic belief! The buzzing
of a fly stuck on flypaper doesn't
spell an agony but a dazzled
self-portrait in the Cyrillic *zh*. A semblance
of alphabet, warmth takes species across the sentence
of the horizon. A landscape shows just the settlers

left behind when their betters escaped to graceful
Asian palm trees. A July morning, faithful
to bedrooms, to shutters, flutters fistfuls
of jasmine banknotes, skipping
the acacia change of its seed pods splitting;
and the air's more diaphanous than a sleeping

beauty's lingerie. Sultry July! The surplus
of the green and the blue—of that threadbare surface
of existence. And a kind of solstice
of the luminary, stopped and splatter-
ing, like Attila before the battered
shield, fills one's orbs. The aforementioned outer

blue flaxlike stuff after all can't spin it
indefinitely. Light simply learns its limit
by means of a body because, within it,
light gets refracted, as at the finish
of too long a road whose beginning few wish
to consider. The finish, though, tends to furnish

butterflies, mallow, hay-scented fever,
a Seym or Oredesz type of river,
its banks strewn with luxuriating figures
of city-folk families; rosy naiads,
their risqué outfits which ignite us;
splutters, splashes; shrill jeremiads

of blue jays thrill pussy willows' bashful
branches obscuring the white parts of bathers
mooning as they wring swimsuits in bushes
upstream; ocher precipices, the pine-needle-
thick aroma, the heat, the nimble
sudden clouds tinting waves with a nickel,

fishlike sheen. All summer reservoirs! Most often
glimmering through foliage, molten
ponds or lakes—those orphan
parts of water surrounded by land; the rustle
of sedge and bulrush, moss-shammied muscles
of snarled snags, tender duckweed, and nascent

yellow nymphaeas, passionless water lilies,
algae or Paradise with no limits
for lines; and a water bug darts the liquid
blue, rather Christlike. And at times a perch is
splashing in order to catch a nervous
glimpse of the world, the way one peers out

a window and reels back afraid of falling.
Summer! The time for the shirt gone flapping,
for the old, animated polemic fumbling
about nightshades, toadstools, or garish,
wart-dotted, poisonous fly agarics;
for the quiet of forest clearings carried

by the peacefulness of their noontime slumber,
when your eyelids get lowered down by languor,
when a bumblebee, if it stung you,

did so because it was too myopic
and simply mistook you for blooming poppies
or a desirable cow dropping

and soared upward, distressed, in an awkward spiral.
The woods look like combs with their teeth in peril.
And a boy's revelation that he is "taller
than the bush though shorter than trees" will scramble
his brain for the rest of it! And a humble
nay! invisible skylark appears to tumble

his trills from on high. Summer! The season of exam cramming,
of formulae, of tossed coins, of a manic
pimpled look in boys, delays caused by panic
in girls; and the colonnade of a college
or bricks of some other seat of knowledge
haunt your dreams. Only fishing rods can abolish

with a swish those worries, the fears and burdens.
And we notice a singlet or else a bodice,
sandals, a bicycle in the grass; we notice
specifically its stainless pedals,
resembling a sergeant's bars or medals.
Indeed, their rubber pads, their metal

spell the future, the century, the whole deal,
Europe, a railroad whose branch, for real,
as though wind-shattered, produces rural
platforms—waterspouts, painted fences,
chickens, hedges, broad peasant faces
of women. In the meantime, each maggot forces

itself out of your tin can, soggy, sluggy,
homesick for its cowshed wall, for its muggy
shade. And then, later, a creaking buggy
lumped with burlap bushels, the clanging harness,
and the track that winds through the fields past harvest
time, and, at a distance, some church's harmless

bottle silhouette, haystacks, barns, stables—mainly
huts with their tarred sloping roofs and lonely
windows for whose sakes only
sunsets exist. And the spokes' shadow upon the shoulder
stretching all the way to the Polish border
runs along like some Fido, or a still bolder

Rover, catching foul mutterings of the driver;
and you stare at your toes or chomp on clover,
your thoughts drifting over to some freckled oval
in the town. And high up, in the very corner
of your eye, it's a crane, and not some infernal
thunderbird. Three cheers for normal

temperature: ten notches below the body's
standard. Three cheers for all things you notice.
For both the closest and the remotest
things. For everything that still matters,
for your shirt's drying tatters, for sunflowers' bent lanterns,
for the faint, distant waltz tune—"Manchurian Mountains."

IV

Summer twilight's fluttering window laces!
Cold cellars packed with milk jugs and lettuce,
a Stalin or a Khrushchev on the latest
news, jammed by cicadas' incessant rattle;
homemade bilberry jelly jars bat the rafters;
lime socks round apple orchards' ankles

look the whiter the darker it gets, like joggers
running beyond what the distance offers;
and farther still loom the real ogres
of full-size elms in the evening's bluing.
Kitchens, vast bottoms and head rugs brewing
something; the hellish fires phewing

in cookstoves' mica peepholes. Suppers on the verandas!
Potato in all its genres and genders,
onions and radishes in their grandest

fashion; tomatoes, dill, cucumbers—
all straight from the garden patch in great numbers;
and, finally, tired of their hide-and-seek, decanters

coated with dust! A soot-rich lantern,
a ballet of shadows dwarfing the wallpaper pattern,
geniuses of this high art, their ardent
admirers; samovar's armor; sugar
that you tell from salt by a fly, and shoo her
off. A nightjar's lonely pitch or super-

cilious frogs voicing every grievance
from their ditch. A silver pitcher glimmers
with your pink oval's distorted grimace,
rustling tabloids, burp-triggered tremors;
from the parlor wafts "Chopsticks," or else some tenor's
record. And Simonides' view on tendons

spares for a moment a keenly placid
stare at the wallpaper or hawthorn's flaccid
ramifications and twists: a glance at
a knee is never enough. The flesh is
dear indeed, since the fabric (bless its
patterns), by hiding the body, lessens

the resistance of skin—free of any pattern—
to one's upward gliding. Meantime, a patina
fogs half-empty tea glasses; prattling
dies; the flame in the lamp, too, suffers
shivers. And later, beneath the covers,
your brand-new pocket compass's needle quivers,

gleaming dully yet pointing north not any
less categorically than many
a prosecutor. Dogs barking, a dropping penny,
creaking joints of old chairs, or is that some invader?—
a sudden cackle in the hen coop, a whistling freight or
cattle train. Yet even these sounds later

cease. And naggingly, softly—even
softer perhaps than your ears are given
to discern—leaves, as countless as souls of all those who lived on
the earth before ourselves, blab something
in their burgeoning dialect; it's sounding
like dark tongues, though their tattered samplings—

smudges, cuneiforms, moon-spun vowels—
are unclear both to you and your wall for hours
as you toss and turn twixt the mounds and hollows
of the mattress, trying in vain to fathom
a sprouting hieroglyph, a phantom
comma, while outdoors the invisible rustling quantum

airs its China-like, powerful yellow anthem.

[1981   /   *Translated by George L. Kline and the author*]

Venetian Stanzas I

To Susan Sontag

I

The wet hitching post of the quay: a sulky hackney
fights off sleep in the twilight, twitching the iron bay
of her mane; napeless gondolas, fiddling numbly
the out-of-sync silence, sway.
As the Moor grows more trusting, words turn the paper darker,
and a hand, short of snapping a neck, though keen on the gothic lace
of a stone kerchief crushed in the palm of Iago,
presses it to its face.

II

The piazza's deserted, the quays abandoned.
The café walls are more crowded than the café inside:
a lute's being strummed by a frescoed, bejeweled maiden
to her similarly decked Said.
Oh, nineteenth century! oh, lure of the East! and oh, clifftop poses
of exiles! and, like leucocytes in the blood,
full moons in the works of bards burning with tuberculosis,
claiming it is with love.

III

At night, there's nothing to do here. No sweet Duses, no arias.
A solo heel's tapping out a basalt street.
Under lamps, your shadowy shuddered alias
like carbonari postpones its hit
and exhales a cloud. At night here we hold soliloquies
to an audience of echoes, whose breath won't warm up, alas,
this resonant marbled fish tank, nor fill it with
anything save steamed glass.

IV

Golden scales of tall windows bring to the rippled surface
wedges of grand piano, bric-a-brac, oils in frames.
That's what's hidden inside, blinds drawn, by perches
or, gills flapping, by breams.
The retina's sudden encounter with a white ceiling's goddess

90

shedding it all but her cobweb bra
makes one dizzy. A doorway's inflamed raw throat is
gaping to utter "Ahhhh."

V

How they flitted their tails here! How they flapped here, breamlike!
How spurning and spawning they streamed to score
the mirror! And how that cleaving, cream-white
bodice's plunge could stir—
like a sirocco that roils the waters. How, in the middle
of the promenade, squalls were turning their pantaloons and skirts
into cabbage soup! Where are they all now—masks, stockings, middies,
harlequins, clowns, flirts?

VI

That's how chandeliers dim at the opera; that's how cupolas
shrink, like medusas, in volume, the tighter night hugs the place;
that's how streets coil and dwindle, like eels; that's how

just-as-populous
squares mimic plaice.
That's how, treating his daughters, Nereus nears us,
pinching the combs from ladies' wind-ravaged curls,
leaving untouched the quays' yellow, nervous,
cheap electrical pearls.

VII

That's how orchestras fade. The city, while words are at it,
is akin to attempts to salvage notes from the silent beat,
and the palazzi, like music stands, stand scattered,
hoarded and poorly lit.
Only up where Perm's citizen sleeps his lasting sleep, a falsetto
star is vibrating through telegraph wires, reaches a minor key.
But the water applauds, and the quay is a hoarfrost settled
down on a do-re-mi.

VIII

And the loaded pupil of Claude, his limbs like half past eleven,
jettisoning his lines to the page's edge
in the struggle to keep all his gray mass level
despite the brandy's siege,

9 1

longs to undress, to cast off his woolen armor,
flop to the bed, press himself to the living, soft
bone's hot mirror from whose amalgam
no finger will scratch him off.

[*1982 / Translated by Jane Ann Miller and the author*]

Venetian Stanzas II

To Gennady Smakov

I

A sleep-crumpled cloud unfurls mealy mizzens.
Slapped by the baker, matte cheeks acquire
a glow. And in pawnbrokers' windows
jewelry catches fire.
Flat garbage barges sail. Like lengthy, supple
sticks run by hot-footed schoolboys along iron grates,
the morning rays strum colonnades, red-brick chimneys, sample
curled seaweed, invade arcades.

II

Dawn takes its time. Cold, naked, pallid marble
thighs of the new Susannah wade waves, being watched with glee
by new elders whose lenses squint, whirr, and gargle
at this bathing. Two-three
doves, launched from some pilaster, are turning
into gulls at the palaces opposite; that's the tax
here for flights over water—or else that's bed linen spurning
the ceiling for what it lacks.

III

Dampness creeps into the bedroom where a sleeping beauty,
dodging the world, draws her shoulder blades in.
That's how quail shrink sometimes at twig-snapping bootsteps,
how angels react to sin.
The window's sentient gauze gets fluttered by both exhaling
and inhaling. A pale, silky foam lashes stiff armchairs and
the mirror—an exit for objects, ailing
locally from their brown dead end.

IV

Light pries your eye—like a shell. Your helix,
in its turn like a shell, gets completely drowned
by the clamor of bells: that's the thirsty cupolas herding,
waterhole- and reflection-bound.
Parting shutters assault your nostrils with coffee, rags and

cinnamon, semen; with something transparent, pink.
And the golden St. George tips his lance at the writhing dragon's
maw, as though drawing ink.

V

Leaving all of the world, all its blue, in the rearguard,
the azure—squared to a weightless mass—
breasts the windowpane's gunport, falling headlong forward,
surrendering to the glass.
A curly-maned cloud pack rushes to catch and strangle
the radiant thief with his blazing hair—
a nor'easter is coming. The town is a crystal jumble
replete with smashed chinaware.

VI

Motorboats, rowboats, gondolas, dinghies, barges—
like odd scattered shoes, unmatched, God-size—
zealously trample pilasters, sharp spires, bridges'
arcs, the look in one's eyes.
Everything's doubled, save destiny, save the very
H_2O. Yet the idle turquoise on high
renders—like any "pro" vote—this world a merry
minority in one's eye.

VII

That's how some rise from the waters, their smooth skin stunning
the knobbly shore—while a flower may sway
in the hand—leaving the slipped dress scanning
the dry land from far away.
That's how they wash you in spray, for the immortals' ardent
perfume of kelp is what marks them from us and scares
pigeons off playing their crazy gambits
on the chessboards of squares.

VIII

I am writing these lines sitting outdoors, in winter,
on a white iron chair, in my shirtsleeves, a little drunk;
the lips move slowly enough to hinder
the vowels of the mother tongue,
and the coffee grows cold. And the blinding lagoon is lapping

at the shore as the dim human pupil's bright penalty
for its wish to arrest a landscape quite happy
here without me.

[*1982 / Translated by Jane Ann Miller and the author*]

Seaward

Darling, you think it's love, it's just a midnight journey.
Best are the dales and rivers removed by force,
as from the next compartment throttles "Oh, stop it, Bernie,"
yet the rhythm of those paroxysms is exactly yours.
Hook to the meat! Brush to the red-brick dentures,
alias cigars, smokeless like a driven nail!
Here the works are fewer than monkey wrenches,
and the phones are whining, dwarfed by to-no-avail.
Bark, then, with joy at Clancy, Fitzgibbon, Miller.
Dogs and block letters care how misfortune spells.
Still, you can tell yourself in the john by the spat-at mirror,
slamming the flush and emerging with clean lapels.
Only the liquid furniture cradles the dwindling figure.
Man shouldn't grow in size once he's been portrayed.
Look: what's been left behind is about as meager
as what remains ahead. Hence the horizon's blade.

[*1983*]

Galatea Encore

As though the mercury's under its tongue, it won't
talk. As though with the mercury in its sphincter,
immobile, by a leaf-coated pond
a statue stands white like a blight of winter.
After such snow, there is nothing indeed: the ins
and outs of centuries, pestered heather.
That's what coming full circle means—
when your countenance starts to resemble weather,
when Pygmalion's vanished. And you are free
to cloud your folds, to bare the navel.
Future at last! That is, bleached debris
of a glacier amid the five-lettered "never."
Hence the routine of a goddess, née
alabaster, that lets roving pupils gorge on
the heart of the color and temperature of the knee.
That's what it looks like inside a virgin.

[*1983*]

Variation in V

"Birds flying high above the retreating army!
Why do you suddenly turn and head toward our enemy,
contrary to the clouds? We are not yet defeated, are we?
True, we are scattered, but we still have some energy."

"Because your numbers diminish. You are less fit to listen
to our songs. You are no more an audience.
Vultures swoop in to replace us, and Valkyries. And the eastern
wind slams the fir horizons like jagged accordions."

"Cuneiform of the beaks! Explosions that sprout a palm tree!
Your tunes will be blown out of the sky, too, by the screaming
                                                    westerly.

We commit them to memory, which is a larger country.
Nobody knows the future, but there is always yesterday."

"Ye-ah! but our life span's shorter. There is no tomb or pyre
for our kind, but chamomile, clover, chicory,
thyme. Your valedictory runs 'Fire! fire! fire!'
We are less comprehensible. That's why we need a victory."

[*1983*]

Letter to an Archaeologist

Citizen, enemy, mama's boy, sucker, utter
garbage, panhandler, swine, *refujew, verrucht;*
a scalp so often scalded with boiling water
that the puny brain feels completely cooked.
Yes, we have dwelt here: in this concrete, brick, wooden
rubble which you now arrive to sift.
All our wires were crossed, barbed, tangled, or interwoven.
Also: we didn't love our women, but they conceived.
Sharp is the sound of the pickax that hurts dead iron;
still, it's gentler than what we've been told or have said ourselves.
Stranger! move carefully through our carrion:
what seems carrion to you is freedom to our cells.
Leave our names alone. Don't reconstruct those vowels,
consonants, and so forth: they won't resemble larks
but a demented bloodhound whose maw devours
its own traces, feces, and barks, and barks.

[*1983*]

Kellomäki

I

Dumped in the dunes snatched from the witless Finns,
a small veneered burg whose walls let one's sneezing fits
be echoed at once by a "Bless you" cabled from Sweden, yet
sporting no ax to split enough wood to heat
up a dwelling. What's more, certain houses aimed
at warming winter itself, using their black walls, and
bred lush flowers at eventide on blue
glass verandah rhomboids or squares; and you,
as though plotting a trip to the polar zone,
were falling asleep there with your thick socks on.

II

Flat, lapping swells of the sea starting with B, in curves,
resembling bleak thoughts about oneself, ran course
onto the empty beach and froze
into wrinkles there. The twitching gauze
of the hawthorn twigs at times would compel one's stark-
naked eye to develop a rippling bark.
Or else a few gulls would issue from the snowy haze
like the curls of the soiled-by-nobody's-fingers page
of a pallid, quietly rustling day,
and no lamp would light up till they flapped away.

III

In small towns one recognizes folk
not by face but by their queuing backs that flock
to the store. And on Saturdays the populace strung out, bound
caravanlike for the sandlike ground
flour, or string bags of smelts rending one's balance sheets.
In a little town usually one eats
the same thing as others. And to distinguish one-
self from the rest, one could only try doodling on
a ruble with its sharp-*cum*-dull hardware
or seeing your things scattered everywhere.

IV

Notwithstanding all that, they were sturdy, those
abandoned matchboxes, stacked in white bundled rows
with two or three rattling, damp heads inside,
which, when feeding a sparrow, huddled to watch the sight,
family-strong, by the window whose trees as well
strove to merge into some baobab whose spill
of branches would overtake the sky's pink hem—
which indeed would happen round 6 p.m.,
when a book was slammed shut; and where once you sat
just two lips were remaining, like that vanished cat.

V

This outermost generosity, this—to denote true worth—
gift to exude, while freezing inside, the warmth
outside was binding tenants and habitats,
and winter considered the drying sheets its own linen. That's
what would stall conversations. A normal laugh
creaked like snow underfoot, leaving prints above
where it powdered the edges of sighs or shy
pronouns with hoarfrost, or turned some "I"
into a crystal, shot with hard turquoise,
that would melt like your tear to reduce the choice.

VI

Did it really happen, all that? And if yes, then why
now disturb the peace of these has-beens by
recalling details, testing shadowy pines by grip
—aping the afterlife (often accurately) when asleep?
Only those who believe (in angels, in roots) will rise
again. And what honestly could Kellomäki prize
as such, save its rail and its schedule of tin-plate links,
whistling from nonexistence, by which these things
would be gobbled up five minutes later, along with blurred
thoughts of love, plus those who have jumped aboard?

VII

Nothing. Winter expanses' slaked lime that would duly grab
from empty suburban platforms its daily grub
was leaving by conifer awnings, with their white load,

the present in its black overcoat, whose broad-
cloth, more sturdy than cheviot and *drap d'or*,
shielded one much better against the future or
the past than the station buffet's dim shack.
There is nothing more permanent than black.
That's what unleashes letters, or Carmen's breast;
that's why opponents of change hit their mattresses fully dressed.

VIII

Never again is that door to endure that key
with its curly goatee, nor is the switch to be
shoved up by one's heaving shoulder, to blind the stale loaf of bread.
This birdhouse has outlived its bird
and its cirrus or cumulous flocks. From time's point of view,
there is no "then," only "there." And "there," through
empty rooms, memory roams like a thief at dusk,
frisking the wardrobe, rummaging through the desk,
knocking over a novel by an unknown
- picking the pocket which is its own.

IX

In mid-life's thick forest, in that dark wood,
man, like a runaway or, better still, a hood,
tends to glance backward: now branches creaking, now water's sound.
But the past is neither that panther nor some greyhound
that leaps onto one's stooped shoulders and, having thrown
the prey to the ground, strangles it in its brown
furry embrace—for its shanks ain't so sweet anymore, alas;
and the liquid, Narcissus-resistant glass
of the river gets icy (the fish, having pondered its
tin-can, flickering silver bits,

X

swims away beforehand). Probably you could state
that you simply were trying to dodge the great
metamorphosis, much as those smelts did. That
every point in space is indeed B-flat,
and a true express, skipping points A, B, and
C, slows down as a rule at the farthest end
of the alphabet, letting the steam out from

its comma-like nostrils. That water, too, runs home
from the basin much faster than it pours in
through a couple of pipes, making the bottom win.

XI

One may nod and admit that the Lobachevsky sleds'
lesson was lost on this terrain. Or let's
say that Finland's asleep, nurturing deep disdains
for ski poles, aluminum-made these days—
that is, better for hands, as they say, for turns;
still, they won't teach a youngster how bamboo burns,
won't evoke palm trees, tsetse flies, fox trot,
monologues of a parrot—i.e., the sort
of parallels where, since the world there ends,
a naked scientist makes naked friends.

XII

In little towns' basements, storing all sorts of scraps,
like snapshots of strangers or playing cards, no maps
are ever kept, as though to block the thresh-
old for fate's bold attempts upon defenseless flesh.
The wallpaper suffices; a populated site
is relieved by its pattern from outer ties
so completely the smoke would in kind decide
to coil back in the chimney, whitewashing its pale façade,
so that the blending of two into one would yield
but a cloudy spot on the laundered field.

XIII

It's irrelevant now to remember your name, or mine.
For your blouse or my waistband will do just fine
to confirm in a trifoliate mirror's splits
that anonymity truly becomes us, fits,
as it does in the end all that's alive, that dwells
on this earth, till the aimless salvo of all one's cells.
Things have their limits—that is, their length
or immobility. And our claim on that piece of land-
scape extended no farther than, should I say,
the woodshed's sharp shadow, which, on a sunny day,

1 0 3

wedged a snowpile. Scanning an alien scene,
let's agree that that wedge can be simply seen
as our common elbow, thrust into the outside;
the elbow that neither of us can bite
or, moreover, kiss. In that sense, I bet,
we really blended—though our standard bed
barely squeaked. For it chose, in its turn, to swell
and become the wide world. In which, on the left as well
there is a door. Which, for all its domestic clout,
may only be good for one's getting out.

[*1985 / Translated by the author*]

Ex Voto

To Jonathan Aaron

Something like a field in Hungary, but without
its innocence. Something like a long river, short
of its bridges. Above, an unutterable umlaut
of eyes staining the view with hurt.
A posthumous vista where words belong
to their echo much more than to what one says.
An angel resembles in the clouds a blond
gone in an Auschwitz of sidewalk sales.
And a stone marks the ground where a sparrow sat.
In shop windows, the palms of the quay foretell
to a mosquito challenging the façade
of a villa—or, better yet, hotel—
his flat future. The farther one goes, the less
one is interested in the terrain.
An aimless iceberg resents bad press:
it suffers a meltdown, and forms a brain.

[*1983*]

Elegy

About a year has passed. I've returned to the place of battle,
to its birds that have learned their unfolding of wings from a subtle
lift of a surprised eyebrow, or perhaps from a razor blade
—wings, now the shade of early twilight, now of stale bad blood.

Now the place is abuzz with trading in your ankles' remnants, bronzes
of sunburnt breastplates, dying laughter, bruises,
rumors of fresh reserves, memories of high treason,
laundered banners with imprints of the many who since have risen.

All's overgrown with people. A ruin's a rather stubborn
architectural style. And the heart's distinction

                                        from a pitch-black cavern
isn't that great; not great enough to fear
that we may collide again like blind eggs somewhere.

At sunrise, when nobody stares at one's face, I often
set out on foot to a monument cast in molten
lengthy bad dreams. And it says on the plinth "Commander
in chief." But it reads "in grief," or "in brief," or "in going under."

[*1985 / Translated by the author*]

The Fly

To Irene and Alfred Brendel

I

While you were singing, fall arrived.
A splinter set the stove alight.
While you were singing, while you flew,
the cold wind blew.

And now you crawl the flat expanse of
my greasy stove top, never glancing
back to whence you arrived last April,
slow, barely able

to put one foot before the other.
So crushing you would be no bother.
Yet death's more boring to a scholar's eye
than torment, fly.

II

While you were singing, while you flew, the leafage
fell off. And water found it easier
to run down to the ground and stare,
disinterested, back into air.

But your eyesight has gone a bit asunder.
The thought of your brain dimming under
your latticed retina—downtrodden,
matte, tattered, rotten—

unsettles one. Yet you seem quite aware of
and like, in fact, this mildewed air of
well-lived-in quarters, green shades drawn.
Life does drag on.

III

Ah, buggie, you've lost all your perkiness;
you look like some old shot-down Junkers,
like one of those scratched flicks that score
            the days of yore.

Weren't you the one who in those times so fatal
droned loud above my midnight cradle,
pursued by crossing searchlights into
            my black-framed window?

Yet these days, as my yellowed finger-
nail mindlessly attempts to fiddle
with your soft belly, you won't buzz with fear
            or hatred, dear.

IV

While you sang on, the gray outside grew grayer.
Damp door-frame joints swell past repair;
drafts numb the soles. This place of mine
            is in decline.

You can't be tempted, though, by the sink's outrageous
slumped pyramids, unwashed for ages,
nor by sweet, shiftless honeymoons
            in sugar dunes.

You're in no mood for that. You're in no mood to
take all that sterling-silver crap. Too good to
let yourself in for all that mess.
            Me too, I guess.

V

Those feet and wings of yours! they're so old-fashioned,
so quaint. One look at them, and one imagines
a cross between Great-grandma's veil
            et la Tour Eiffel

—the nineteenth century, in short. However,
by likening you to this and that, my clever

pen ekes out of your sorry end
a profit and

prods you to turn into some fleshless substance,
thought-like, unpalpable—into an absence
ahead of schedule. Your pursuer
admits: it's cruel.

VI

What is it that you muse of there?
Of your worn-out though uncomputed derring-
do orbits? Of six-legged letters,
your printed betters,

your splayed Cyrillic echoes, often
spotted by you in days gone by on open
book pages, and—misprints abhorring—
fast you'd be soaring

off. Now, though, since your eyesight lessens,
you spurn those black-on-white curls, tresses,
releasing them to real brunettes, their ruffles,
chignons, thick afros.

VII

While you were singing, while you flew, the birds went
away. Brooks, too, meander free, unburdened
of stickleback. Groves flaunt see-throughs—no takers.
The cabbage acres

crackle with cold, though tightly wrapped for winter,
and an alarm clock, like a time bomb, whimpers
tick-tock somewhere; its dial's dim and hollow:
the blast won't follow.

Apart from that, there are no other sounds.
Rooftop by rooftop, light rebounds
back into cloud. The stubble shrivels.
It gives one shivers.

VIII

And here's just two of us, contagion's carriers.
Microbes and sentences respect no barriers,
afflicting all that can inhale or hear.
Just us two here—

your tiny countenance pent up with fear
of dying, my sixteen, or near,
stones playing at some country squire—
plus autumn's mire.

Completely gone, it seems, your precious buzzer.
To time, though, this appears small bother—
to waste itself on us. Be grateful
that it's not hateful,

IX

that it's not squeamish. Or that it won't care
what sort of shoddy deal, what kind of fare
it's getting stuck with in the guise of
some large nose-divers

or petty ones. Your flying days are over.
To time, though, ages, sizes never
appear distinguishable. And it poses
alike for causes

as for effects, by definition. Even—
nay! notably—if those are given
in miniature: like to cold fingers,
small change's figures.

X

So while you were off there, busy flirting
around the half-lit light bulb's flicker,
or, dodging me, amidst the rafters,
it—time—stayed rather

the same as now, when you acquire the stature
—due to your impotence and to your posture

toward myself—of pallid dust. Don't ponder,
decrepit, somber,

that time is my ally, my partner.
Look, we are victims of a common pattern.
I am your cellmate, not your warden.
There is no pardon.

XI

Outside, it's fall. A rotten time for bare
carnelian twigs. Like in the Mongol era,
the gray, short-legged species messes
with yellow masses,

or just makes passes. And yet no one cares
for either one of us. It seems what pairs us
is some paralysis—that is, your virus.
You'd be desirous

to learn how fast one catches this, though lucid,
indifference and sleep-inducing
desire to pay for stuff so global
with its own obol.

XII

Don't die! Resist! Crawl! though you don't feel youthful.
Existence is a bore when useful,
for oneself specially—when it spells a bonus.
A lot more honest

is to hound calendars' dates with a presence
devoid of any sense or reasons,
making a casual observer gather:
life's just another

word for nonbeing and for breaking rules. Were
you younger, my eyes'd scan the sphere
where all that is abundant. You are,
though, old and near.

XIII

So here's two of us. Outside, rain's flimsy
beak tests the windowpanes, and in a whimsy
crosshatches the landscape: its model.
You are immobile.

Still, there's us two. At least, when you expire,
I mentally will note the dire
event, thus mimicking the loops so boldly
spun by your body

in olden times, when they appeared so witless.
Death too, you know, once it detects a witness,
less firmly puts full-stops, I bet,
than tête-à-tête.

XIV

I hope you're not in pain, just lonely.
Pain takes up space; it therefore could only
creep toward you from outside, sneak near
you from the rear

and cup you fully—which implies, I reckon,
my palm that's rather busy making
these sentences. Don't die as long as
the worst, the lowest

still can be felt, still makes you twitch. Ah, sister!
to hell with the small brain's disaster!
A thing that quits obeying, dammit,
like that stayed moment,

XV

is beautiful in its own right. In other
words, it's entitled to applause (well, rather,
to the reversed burst), to extend its labor.
Fear's but a table

of those dependencies that dryly beckon
one's atrophy to last an extra second.

1 1 2

And I for one, my buzzy buddy,
    I am quite ready

    to sacrifice one of my own. However,
    now such a gesture is an empty favor:
    quite shot, my Shiva, is your motor;
        your torpor's mortal.

                    XVI
In memory's deep faults, great vaults, among her
    vast treasures—spent, dissolved, disowned or
    forgotten (on the whole, no miser
        could size them, either

    in ancient days or, moreover, later)—
    amidst existence's loose change and glitter,
your near-namesake, called the Muse, now makes a
        soft bed, dear *Musca*

    domestica, for your protracted
rest. Hence these syllables, hence all this prattling,
    this alphabet's cortege: ink trailers,
        upsurges, failures.

                    XVII
Outside, it's overcast. Designed for friction
    against the furniture, my means of vision
    gets firmly trained on the wallpaper.
        You're in no shape to

    take to the highest its well-traveled pattern,
    to stun up there, where prayers pummel
    clouds, feeble seraphs with the notion
        of repetition

    and rhythm—seen senseless in their upper
    realms, being rooted in the utter
    despair for which these cloudborne insects
        possess no instincts.

                    1 1 3

XVIII

What will it end like? In some housefly heaven?
an apiary or, say, hidden
barn, where above spread cherry jam a heavy
and sleepy bevy

of your ex-sisters slowly twirls, producing
a swish the pavement makes when autumn's using
provincial towns? Yet push the doors:
a pale swarm bursts

right past us back into the world—out! out!—
enveloping it in their white shroud
whose winter-like shreds, snatches, forms
—whose swarm confirms

XIX

(thanks to this flicker, bustling, frantic)
that souls indeed possess a fabric
and matter, and a role in landscape,
where even blackest

things in the end, for all their throttle,
too, change their hue. That the sum total
of souls surpasses any tribe.
That color's time

or else the urge to chase it—quoting
the great Halicarnassian—coating
rooftops *en face*, hills in profile
with its white pile.

XX

Retreating from their pallid whirlwind,
shall I discern you in their winged
(a priori, not just Elysian)
a-swirling legion,

and you swoop down in your familiar fashion
onto my nape, as though you missed your ration

of mush that thinks itself so clever?
          Fat chance. However,

     having kicked off the very last—by eons—
you'll be the last among those swarming millions.
     Yet if you're let in on a scene so private,
          then, local climate

                    XXI
     considered—so capricious, flippant—
next spring perhaps I'll spot you flitting
     through skies into this region, rushing
          back home. I, sloshing

through mud, might sigh, "A star is shooting,"
     and vaguely wave to it, assuming
          some zodiac mishap—whereas
          there, quitting spheres,

     that will be your winged soul, a-flurry
     to join some dormant larva buried
          here in manure, to show its nation
               a transformation.

[*1986 / Translated by Jane Ann Miller and the author*]

Belfast Tune

Here's a girl from a dangerous town.
    She crops her dark hair short
so that less of her has to frown
    when someone gets hurt.

She folds her memories like a parachute.
    Dropped, she collects the peat
and cooks her veggies at home: they shoot
    here where they eat.

Ah, there's more sky in these parts than, say,
    ground. Hence her voice's pitch,
and her stare stains your retina like a gray
    bulb when you switch

hemispheres, and her knee-length quilt
    skirt's cut to catch the squall.
I dream of her either loved or killed
    because the town's too small.

[*1986*]

Afterword

I

The years are passing. On the palace's pumice façade appears
a crack. The eyeless seamstress's thread finally spears the midget
eye of the needle. And the Holy Family, the features drawn, severe,
comes half a millimeter more close to Egypt.

The bulk of the visible world consists of living types.
The streets are lit with a bright, extraneous
light. And at night an astronomer reckons, straining his
eyes, the total of sparkling tips.

II

I am no longer able to recall where or when events
occurred. This one, or any other.
Yesterday? A few years ago? On a garden bench?
In the air? In the water? Was I the matter?

And the event itself—an explosion or, say, a flood,
the lights of the Kuzbas derricks or some betrayal—
can't recall anything either, burying thus the trail
of myself or of those who either were saved or fled.

III

This, presumably, means that we are now in league
with life. That I, too, have become a segment
of that rustling matter whose fabric's bleach
infects one's skin with its neutral pigment.

In profile I, too, now can hardly be set
apart from some wrinkle, domino, patchwork, fig leaf,
fractions or wholes, causes or their effects—
from all that can be ignored, coveted, stood in fear of.

IV

Touch me—and you'll touch dry burdock stems,
the dampness intrinsic to evenings in late Marchember,

the stone quarry of cities, the width of steppes,
those who are not alive but whom I remember.

Touch me—and you'll disturb a little that which does
exist regardless of me, obviously in the process
not trusting me, my overcoat, my face—
that in whose book we are always losses.

                                   v

I am speaking to you, and it's not my fault
if you don't hear. The sum of days, by slugging
on, blisters eyeballs; the same goes for vocal cords.
My voice may be muffled but, I should hope, not nagging.

All the better to hear the crowing of a cockerel, the tick-tocks
in the heart of a record, its needle's patter;
all the better for you not to notice when my talk stops,
as Red Riding Hood didn't mutter to her gray partner.

   [*1986 / Translated by Jamey Gambrell and the author*]

At Karel Weilink's Exhibition

To Ada Stroeve

I

Nearly a landscape. The full figure count,
appearing in it, gradually flees
the influx of bare statues. Like a coal
turned inside out, the marble's blondish, bleached,
and the locale seems northern. A plateau;
the cabbage tousled by a polar blast.
It's all so very horizontal that
no one will clasp you to an anxious breast.

II

Perhaps—this is the future. Backdrop of
repentance. An old colleague's vengeance. One
distinct yet muffled expletive, "Get out!"
A martial artist's unexpected veer.
And this—the future's town. Your lidless eyes
stay glued to rampant garden growth, alert,
like lizards scanning tropical hotel
façades. And skyscrapers even more.

III

It's possibly the past. Despair's last swoon,
its limit. Common summit. Verbs that wait
in line to view the preterit entombed.
A storm of crumpled velvet settled, passed.
And here's the past's dominion. Paths grown dense
while straying in reality. Lagoons
preserving lapsed reflections. Eggshells glimpsed
externally by yolk's unscrambled pools.

IV

Clearly—perspective. Calendar of sorts.
Or rather, from inflamed and swollen throats,
a tunnel sunk to psychological
beyonds, unfettered by our features. For
the voice, acquainted better with the thick

and thin of failure's landscape than is sight,
the greater evil's handier to pick—
it reckons on the echo's kind response.

V

Perhaps it's—still life. Far away it seems
that everything within the stretchers is
part dead and certainly immobile. Clouds.
A river, over which in circles flies
a bird. A plain, unable quite to stage
a transmutation, dons another shape,
becomes the prey of canvas, postcard, page,
the vindication Ptolemy awaits.

VI

Perhaps it's—tidal zebras or a half
a tiger hide. A hybrid barricade
and rumpled dress that licks the supple calves
of balusters immune to sunburn; and
the time approaches evening. Stifling heat;
a lone mosquito's stubborn solo, whose
pitch hoists the sweaty hammer from its soft and sweet
forge, dies amidst the bedroom's loud applause.

VII

Perhaps—the decoration for a set.
A staging of the classic "Cause's Rude
Indifference to Parting from Effect."
In greeting creature comforts singers prove
less gentle than myopic; "fa" resounds
a short-lived "far." And, trembling, brilliant, slight,
above the wire of notes like faucet drops,
the moonspun trill of the soprano glides.

VIII

Clearly—a portrait, but without a lick
of varnish. Dark, a subtly surfaced pall
whose earthy tints quite naturally arrest
the eye—of one who's up against the wall.
A ways away, a compromise with white,

1 2 0

Olympians amass in storm clouds, sense
the stare aimed at their backs, the inside-out-
ward gaze, the painter's—i.e., the suicide's.

IX

Which is the essence of self-portraiture.
A step aside from one's own flesh and frame,
the profile of a footstool kicked toward
you, a long view on life when dues are paid.
This, then, is "mastery": ability
to not take fright at the procedure of
nonbeing—as another form of one's
own absence, having drawn it straight from life.

[*1984 / Translated by Jamey Gambrell*]

"Slave, Come to My Service!"

I

"Slave, come to my service!" "Yes, my master. Yes?"
"Quick, fetch my chariot, hitch up the horses: I'll drive to the palace!"
"Drive to the palace, my master. Drive to the palace.
The King will be pleased to see you, he will be benevolent to you."
"No, slave. I won't go to the palace!"
"Don't, my master. Don't go to the palace.
The King will send you on a faraway expedition,
down the unknown road, through hostile mountains;
day and night he will make you experience pain and hardship."

II

"Slave, come to my service!" "Yes, my master. Yes?"
"Fetch water, pour it over my hands: I am to eat my supper."
"Eat your supper, my master. Eat your supper.
Frequent meals gladden one's heart. Man's supper
is the supper of his god, and clean hands catch the eye of Shamash."
"No, slave. I won't eat my supper!"
"Don't eat your supper, master. Don't eat your supper.
Drink and thirst, food and hunger
never leave man alone, let alone each other."

III

"Slave, come to my service!" "Yes, my master. Yes?"
"Quick, fetch my chariot, hitch up the horses: I'll go for a ride in
the country."
"Do that, my master. Do that. A carefree wanderer
always fills his belly, a stray dog always
finds a bone, a migrating swallow is especially skilled in nesting,
a wild donkey finds the grass in the driest desert."

This text dates back to the eleventh or tenth century B.C. *and is known among Sumerian scholars as "The Dialogue of Pessimism." In antiquity it was regarded as a philosophical text; now some argue that it is, rather, a skit. For my translation, I used two interlinear renditions: one was taken from* Babylonian Wisdom Literature *by W. G. Lambert (Oxford, 1960); the other, from* Ancient Near Eastern Texts Relating to the Old Testament, *by James B. Pritchard (Princeton, 1955).* —J.B.

"No, slave. I won't go for a ride in the country."
"Don't go, my master. Don't bother.
The lot of a wanderer is always dicey.
A stray dog loses its teeth. The nest
of a migrating swallow gets buried in plaster.
Naked earth is a wild donkey's bedding."

IV

"Slave, come to my service!" "Yes, my master. Yes?"
"I feel like starting a family, like begetting children."
"Good thinking, my master. Start a family, start a family.
Who has children secures his name, repeated in posthumous prayers."
"No, slave. I won't start a family, I won't have children!"
"Don't start it, my master. Don't have them.
A family is like a broken door, its hinge is creaking.
Only a third of one's children are healthy; two-thirds always sickly."
"So, should I start a family?" "Don't start a family.
Who starts a family wastes his ancestral house."

V

"Slave, come to my service!" "Yes, my master. Yes?"
"I shall yield to my enemy;
in the court, I'll stay silent before my detractors."
"Right, my master, right. Yield to your enemy;
keep silence, my master, before your detractors."
"No, slave! I won't be silent, and I won't yield!"
"Don't yield, my master, and don't be silent.
Even if you don't open your mouth at all
your enemies will be merciless and cruel to you, as well as numerous."

VI

"Slave, come to my service!" "Yes, my master. Yes?"
"I feel like doing some evil, eh?"
"Do that, my master. By all means, do some evil.
For how otherwise can you stuff your belly?
How, without doing evil, can you dress yourself warmly?"
"No, slave. I shall do no evil!"
"Evildoers are either killed, or flayed alive and blinded,
or blinded and flayed alive and thrown into a dungeon."

"Slave, come to my service!" "Yes, my master. Yes?"
"I'll fall in love with a woman." "Fall in love, my master. Fall in love!
Who falls in love with a woman forgets his griefs and sorrows."
"No, slave. I won't fall in love with a woman!"
"Don't love, my master. Don't love.
Woman is a snare, a trap, a dark pit.
Woman is a sharp steel blade slitting man's throat in darkness."

VIII

"Slave, come to my service!" "Yes, my master. Yes?"
"Quick, fetch water to wash my hands: I am to make an offering
                                                       to my god."
"Make an offering, make an offering.
Who makes offerings to his god fills his heart with riches;
he feels generous, and his purse is open."
"No, slave. I won't make an offering!"
"Rightly so, my master. Rightly so!
Can you really train your god to follow you like a doggy?
All the time he demands obedience, rituals, sacrifices!"

IX

"Slave, come to my service!" "Yes, my master. Yes?"
"I'll invest with the interest, I will loan for the interest."
"Yes, invest with the interest, make loans for the interest.
Who does so preserves his own; his profit, though, is enormous."
"No, slave, I won't lend and I won't invest!"
"Don't invest, my master. Don't lend.
To lend is like loving a woman; to receive, like siring bad children:
people always curse those whose grain they eat.
They'll resent you or try to reduce your profit."

X

"Slave, come to my service!" "Yes, my master. Yes?"
"I shall do a good deed for my nation!"
"Very good, my master, very good. You do that!
Who does good deeds for his nation has his name in Marduk's
                                                       gold signet."
"No, slave. I won't do a good deed for my nation."
"Don't do that, my master. Don't bother.

Get up and stroll across ancient ruins,
scan the skulls of simple folk and nobles:
which one of them was a villain, which one a benefactor?"

XI
"Slave, come to my service!" "Yes, my master. Yes?"
"If all this is so, then what is good?"
"To have your neck broken and my neck broken,
to be thrown into a river —that's what is good!
Who is so tall as to reach the heavens?
Who so broad as to embrace plains and mountains?"
"If that's so, I should kill you, slave: I'd rather you go before me."
"And does my master believe that he can survive for three days
                                          without me?"

[1987]

In Italy

To Roberto and Fleur Calasso

I, too, once lived in a city whose cornices used to court
clouds with statues, and where a local *penseur*, with his
                                              shrill "Pervért!
Pervért!" and the trembling goatee, was mopping
avenues; and an infinite quay was rendering life myopic.

These days evening sun still blinds the tenements' domino.
But those who have loved me more than themselves are no
longer alive. The bloodhounds, having lost their quarry,
with vengeance devour the leftovers—herein their very

strong resemblance to memory, to the fate of all things. The sun
sets. Faraway voices, exclamations like "Scum!
Leave me alone!"—in a foreign tongue, but it stands to reason.
And the world's best lagoon with its golden pigeon

coop gleams sharply enough to make the pupil run.
At the point where one can't be loved any longer, one,
resentful of swimming against the current and too perceptive
of its strength, hides himself in perspective.

[*1985 / Translated by the author*]

In Memoriam

The thought of you is receding like a chambermaid given notice.
No! like a railway platform, with block-lettered DVINSK or TATRAS.
But odd faces loom in, shivering and enormous,
also terrains, only yesterday entered into the atlas,
thus filling up the vacuum. None of us was well suited
for the status of statues. Probably our blood vessels
lacked in hardening lime. "Our family," you'd have put it,
"gave the world no generals, or—count our blessings—
great philosophers." Just as well, though: the Neva's surface
can't afford yet another reflection, brimming with "mediogres."
What can remain of a mother with all her saucepans
in the perspective daily extended by her son's progress?
That's why the snow, this poor man's marble, devoid of muscle power,
melts, blaming empty brain cells for their not so clever
locks, for their failure to keep the fashion in which you,
                                                    by putting powder
on your cheek, had meant to look forever.
What is left is to shield the skull, with raised arms, against
                                                    idle glances,
and the throat, with the lips' nonstop "She has died, she has died,"
                                                    while endless
cities rip the retinal sacs with lances
clanging loud like returning empties.

[*1985 / Translated by the author*]

Gorbunov and Gorchakov

Gorbunov and Gorchakov

"So, what'd you dream of this time, Gorbunov?"
"Oh, mushrooms mostly." "Mushrooms? Curious.
Again?" "Again." "You really make me laugh."
"And why is that? It's pretty serious.
Regularity in sleep's the stuff
the doctors seem to think is curing us."
"No offense—but you've not had enough
of all this fungus?" "Well, up here I guess
it's all I've got." "In Leningrad we have
so many dreams, but 'mushroom' clearly is

the one you're wedded to." "And what
are all you Leningraders dreaming, then?"
"Well, it depends. Of concerts forested
with bows. Of avenues and alleys. Men—
just faces. (All in all, they're fragmented.)
The Neva, bridges. Or a page I can
discern—although the nurse collects, come bed-
time, all our specs—without my glasses on!"
"That dream's too much for these dull eyes to read!"
"And then I dream myself back here again."

"Who needs real life? Just take a look around.
Now there's a dream. The day's gratuitous.
The dawn dims dreams like that. And how you groan
with rage when you're awakened. —Mickiewicz!
Try and keep it down, okay? —For one
of those I'd gladly slumber through to dusk,
miss supper, too . . ." "Sometimes my dreams are prone
to birds, to bullfinches, a kid who is
leaping puddles—and it's me . . ." "What's wrong?
Go on!" "I think I've got the flu. Do these

things interest you at all? What for?" "Beats me.
Just do." "I dream of childhood: sneaking through
an attic with my pals, just two or three
of us. And of old age—nowhere to go
to shake off *that* unholy mess, I see.
Old man, young brat . . ." "Bleak apposition, no?"
"Oh, Gorbunov, that's pure stupidity.
These dreams are only manufactured so
as to give our nights variety,
to give day's heritage a jolt or two."

"Now there's a conundrum, this 'heritage.'
A question, though, you can't ignore:
what *of* old age? You hardly act your age,
or even have gray hairs." "Or ever snore
quite like Babanov on the window ledge?
Or ever, like Mickiewicz does, resort
to bustling and garbled badinage?
What'd we get imagination for
if not to use it pump-like to discharge
old age into our dreams." "Forgive me, Gor-

chakov, but in that case it can't be true
it's you you're dreaming of." "The Crosses was
constructed for stone-headed fools like you.
And there they'll keep you living under glass!
So tell me who I'm dreaming of . . . yoo hoo!"
"Gor-kiewicz . . . or Gor-banov, no?" "You ass!
You're crazy, Gorbunov." "The face I knew—
as yours—with their gray hair. My friend, for us
there's daily self-deceit aplenty to
disgust." "Next they'll sew your pocket closed."

"I sport pajamas with no underwear
on as it is." "At times I see a ring
of burning logs, and stoves . . ." "A real one there!
Streets, conversations. Simply things. The string
and woodwind sections playing as a pair.

And women. And, perhaps, a spicy fling."
"Just yesterday I dreamt of silverware
for six." "Do they amount to anything—
your dreams—or whirl like chaos everywhere?"
"Some seem coherent, some just menacing."

"Herr Freud says we're imprisoned by our dreams."
"I've always heard that we are slaves to habit.
Apparently you're stumped by what this means."
"No, I can see the page on which I read it."
"Freud was a liar." "Liars come in reams . . .
Now let's suppose you're in the mood to have it—"
"You mean the thing in pants?" "Or out, it seems
—but dream your face with titmice gnawing at it.
No gossip's more explicit than your dreams."
"And so this brings us to your mushrooms, *ibid*."

"They're just like islands. (Mushrooms even sprout
like little islands.) And the same can stand
for streets and alleys, dead ends, words. Throughout
our lives we speak in spurts, or tend to. And
between the spurts, like silence, all about
is grass. But you can touch them with your hand!
And so they have unbounded rights, and what
sustains the solid ground on which I stand
seems as unsteady as a rocking float
the Neva's currents bear away from land."

"Then you're just like those fishermen who face
the water, watching where their bobbins go,
for hour after hour lodged in place?
I've got it right?" "So far, exactly so."
"And, during supper, fashioning new shapes
of lures, light-hearted, in the evening's glow?"
"And hiding mealworms in my tackle case!"
"You'll be locked in here forever." "No!
Why are you aggravating me?" "Because
my name is Gorchakov, as well you know."

Gorbunov and Gorchakov

"Had supper?" "Yeah, some vegetables, a dish
of Jell-O." "Things keep looking up, I see.
And what's outside?" "The starry fields." "What's this?
Another Galileo, doubtlessly!"
"With the departure of Aquarius
around the twentieth of February, we
see Pisces in ascendancy, the fish-
sign pledging rivers will again run free."
"And what about the earth?" "The earth?" "Well, yes.
What's down below?" "That alley edged with trees."

"You know what, Gorbunov? Your case is sad:
a neo-Newton-*cum*-analysand.
There's this guy Khomutov, who says amid
the lockups' retching, histrionics, and
the noise, 'Name's Hamilton, and I'm not mad.'
And yet he snores just like a Khariton."
"Erecting all our seaports, Peter had
to bring the Teutons in to get it done.
The names were harder than the work they did.
Our Khomutov may be a Hamilton."

"The heater's on, and yet I feel a chill."
"Don't lean against the window, then." "Why not?
You think your shiny pets above us will . . . ?"
"Are you convinced?" "Oh no, I'm full of doubt:
I see the snowdrifts and the lane. That's all."
"Look over there: Aquarius is out,
he's bending with the Dipper." "We'd do well
to have a telescope. You wouldn't shout
so much." "A telescope! In here? Like hell!"
"What *are* you getting so worked up about?"

"You've put your filthy feet up on my cot.
At least you could have taken off those mold-
y slippers first." "I'm cold. You know, the thought
devoted to your chanterelles has told

on me. I'm chilled down to my bones without
my slippers on. And so you shouldn't scold."
"Did Freud dream up such progress? That I doubt.
And progress is a thing we should uphold:
the activist, he dreams a rainy wood;
the passivist contracts a nasty cold."

"Your chanterelles are hazards to the sane.
Beware, they're far from harmless, Gorbunov.
How much importance do you give to them?"
"As much as I give love." "And what is love?"
"The end to loneliness." "The very end?"
"It's being able, once, to stand above
the bed and, by just bending over in
the silence, with your hands, brow, breath, touch life."
"What are you staring at? The stars? The lane?"
"The opposite of empty narrative."

"Toss me an apple." "Catch." "Just tell me this:
what are your mushrooms, if you know at all?"
"Whenever I see toadstools in the grass
or forest floor, I find that I recall,
well, love. It's in the mind, or blood perhaps,
for always like an echo, dim but real,
I feel it." "That's just habit and, alas,
the mind's penchant for going general."
"The hands do that. Upstairs what's striking is
a total dearth of the habitual."

"So in the darkness of your sleep you dream
of chanterelles?" "Yes, constantly." "And so
you dream of love?" "It's all the same . . . You seem
to think that's strange." "Not strange. It's sinful, though.
Yes, sinful, and, to tell the truth, I deem
the whole thing utterly disgraceful." "No!"
"What's got you smirking now?" "You're such a scream."
"Toss me an apple, won't you?" "Sure, although
you'll never catch all that the mushrooms mean."
" 'Mushrooms'? That's polygamy, you know.

There now! I planted that one on your chin!
The bitterness I feel is manifest
in my reproach." "You tell me it's a sin,
but sin is something punished in the flesh,
and how can Gorbunov be punished when
life's agonies lie focused in his breast
as in a prism? Is the future clear
of obstacles?" "Apparently we're guests
at someone's wake." "Apparently my grin
makes me, today at least, an optimist."

"And the Last Judgment?" "That's just memory
in flashback, like a film. Why magnify
Apocalypse? Come on, what's it to me?
Five months spent in a wasteland. Merely five.
Well, I've blown half my life and I would be
content to sleep with mushrooms till I die.
I know, however, when and where I'll flee
before the Fiery Angel of the Sky . . ."
"Pain crushes pride." "No, not a bit. The tree
of pride sucks up our suffering to thrive."

"You're saying you don't fear the dark?" "It has
its landmarks, and with some of them I am
acquainted rather well." "You swear it does?"
"Plenty. Just give a whistle and they'll come."
"Vanity's mother is inventiveness."
"I doubt the wisdom of that apothegm.
A man's soul never feels the loss of space."
"And of dead creatures would you say the same?"
"I think the soul, while living in this place,
assumes the features of its mortal frame."

CANTO 3
Gorbunov in the Night

It's night. The hospital. The hostile ground . . .
This hardly qualifies for tragedy . . .
Besides, the tougher life a mortal's found,

the smoother things will seem on Judgment Day
for this soul, when the sentences resound.
I feel, when life is really wretched, I
could tolerate with ease a second round.
That's why inside the man—a child, and why
the mushrooms got me here, though all they meant
to me is out there somewhere, far away.

I dream of chanterelles, but never dream
now of my wife . . . It seems that's as it ought
to be. As fabric tears where thinnest. Some
truth in—got her pregnant, guess I thought
I'd make her stay. The reasoning of a bum.
Apparently I finally bottomed out.
Don't know about my soul, although I am
about my eardrums' health in little doubt:
I hear Babanov now—he's humming, comb
in mouth; a sheet is rustling on a cot.

I hear a voice amid these nighttime sounds—
not auricular hallucination, for
the ear's outfitted even with defense
against the pressure at the ocean's floor.
Besides, I'm contradicted by its sense,
that voice—consistent, hollow, sure.
Whose voice is it? Can't be my wife's. And since
persistently the supernatural world
stays silent as my wife, it can't be saints.
Oh, how I wish I had my muffler here!

It's night. The hospital. The lane, the drifts
of snow. An alder hums, contesting heaven.
Kike-wise the night nurse in the hallway lifts
his Jewish telescope and peers in, laughing.
My pupil's shrinking, shrinking—it resists
the bed contracting on me like a coffin.
And my blood bubbles like bicarbonates.
My ankle freezes as it comes uncovered.
My mind divides the way a microbe splits
and in the silence multiplies forever.

1 3 7

Yes, two of us, before the altar. Inasmuch . . .
She left, and somewhat irritated, maimed,
I crave an interlocutor to match.
Yes, there were two. Indeed, so two remained.
Relieving February, enter March:
that's how the altar, in its turn remind-
ing one of guardsmen, like the still night-watch,
because of how the calendar's designed,
obstructs the silence, my assault on which
creates another force field here inside.

She left. I am possessed by, I possess
myself. Myself? Well, maybe I should call
for Gorchakov? . . . Hey, Gorchakov! . . . I guess
the bed-bell's rung. But is it, after all,
so senseless for one pair of vying lips,
especially without a music hall,
to sing as two? I watch them as they press
together, syllable by syllable.
I am—a circle cleaved. Thus, more or less,
we're magnets, horseshoe-shaped, identical.

Night. Night. My lips performing a duet.
You think that it's too good for you? I say
that there's a special coziness in it.
It is a contradiction, yes, but they
are close. Almost a family when bit.
And all the more so in a brief display.
The upper lip is like a groom, to wit:
The lower lip is like his fiancée.
But that which splits in two will surely split
into two hundred just as easily.

And everything that's been twofold is then
accountable, is then no longer moot.
The solitude dilemma's answered when
it's split. Despair divides my soul like wood—
in two—and yet it's not that I remain
beside it *tête-à-tête*. Two-souledness would

1 3 8

seem atheistic, but it's not the flame
that logs require: the inverse makes it hot.

O God in heaven, if you're so designed
that you can listen to two voices blast
at once from but one set of lips and find
in them not noise but strife between the past
and future, raise to you my coughing mind
and plant its microbes where your light is cast.
Divide among them with your mighty hand
the sum of these convulsive thoughts and days.
And leave the fraction of me left behind
to triumph over silence then, at least.

But if I really need a listener, send,
O Lord, without delay, a denizen
of heaven down to me. I won't pretend
to be superior to him in sin
or sarcasm. He wouldn't comprehend
them anyway. But if that's out, well then,
let cherubs and not Gorchakov ascend
above the filthy hole they keep me in,
and, like your blessing, circle to the end
above the sobbing and surveillant men.

CANTO 4

Gorchakov and the Doctors

"Well, Gorchakov, make your report." "You mean
on Gorbunov?" "Of course, on Gorbunov."
"His mental operation is, when seen
in toto, dialectical, but half
of all his statements clearly contravene
the Party's views, and several, as to both
events and things, are new to us." "A sign
his blood is not nitrogenous enough,
and thus we see disintegration in
the patient's self-controlling operative."

"His chin is puffy, asymmetrical.
His brows close-knit and thick. His nose is mapped
with intersecting veins that twist and swell."
"Bad kidneys, I should say." "His forehead, wrapped
in compresses and asymmetrical as well,
is like a knot of arteries that snapped.
His weakness and his god's the chanterelle.
With women, you might say he's handicapped.
'The inner world is made majestical;
the outer, correspondingly, is scrapped'—

now there's your standard Gorbunov-ish line.
In regular pronouncements more or less
like this one, one can easily divine
all his wrongheaded—his non-Partyness."
"A leftward shift. He's out to undermine
our trusted Marxist principles." "There is
too little evidence." "Well, does he whine
at atmospheric changes?" "Does he miss
the fairer sex a lot?" "No, there he's fine,
his manner, really, the antithesis,

in fact, of a . . . oh, what's it called? I say . . ."
"Composure, Gorchakov." "A paramour."
And how's he down below? . . . *Déshabillé*,
his privates . . ." "Strictly business. Out the door,
the can, and back again three times a day.
If you'll forgive my crudeness." "Say no more.
And have a glass of water." "Water?" "Hey!
You were expecting cognac?" "No! I'm sure
I never touch the stuff!" "Then tell us why
you licked your lips when I began to pour."

"I'm not sure why . . . Some memory of water."
"Water? What?" "I can't remember what.
I'm sorry . . ." "Supper, did you drink a lot, or—"
"No . . . you've tied my mind up in a knot . . .
But wait! I see . . . a man . . . and sands like Tartar
hordes a-whirling round . . . He hasn't got
a drop to drink; he's thin; it's hotter, hotter . . .

1 4 0

Sun is at . . . what do you call it . . . at
the zenith. Hostile ground. It's getting harder
now to see. Then, boom, a well . . ." "Proceed!"

"Then everything again is empty, dead!
The well, well, disappeared with all the rest . . ."
"Gorchakov? What's wrong?" "I've lost my head.
I'm sorry. I admit I was impressed
when with such majesty today he made
his full idealism manifest."
"Who? Gorbunov?" "Of course! Who else? He said . . .
I . . . er . . . oh, please forgive me, I digress."
"No, no. Don't worry. Please, do go ahead."
"I'm too involved with Gorbunov, I guess.

Non-Party! *That's* what's wrong with him!
Indeed! And when the temperature approaches
zero, he moves to that end of the room . . .
well . . . toward the heater . . . to the left." "Prodigious!"
"Is he at all religious?" "Is a hymn?
He is exceedingly relig-religious!
Sometimes I am afraid the day will come
he'll kneel and summon God from heaven's reaches
down to bless the sanitorium."
"Well, being so non-Party, sure he's anxious."

"So: 'deviations to the left.' " "Ha-ha!"
"Dear colleague, what's so funny?" "Just the plain
stupidity of what you said just now.
Observe: the heater, as we ascertain,
is left of Gorchakov, it surely . . ." "Ah,
is right of Gorbunov! Like king and queen
in chess. Well, to be safe we won't withdraw
the other option but instead maintain
the presence of the two phenomena."
"What good's a song without a good refrain?"

"Well, Doctors, do we have our diagnosis?
Staple this; now, Gorchakov, please sign
here, at the bottom." "Haven't got my glasses."

"Won't mine do?" "They might. Let's see: 'We find
some deviations to the left at places' . . .
That's for sure! . . . 'and to the right' . . . That's fine!
They're both correct. We'll fix these lordly asses.
Either we'll exterminate their kind,
or—" "Thank you, Comrade Gorchakov. It pleases
us to let you off at Eastertime."

"I thank you, friends. Mere thanks don't say enough
to thank in full . . . What now? Should I salaam?
Where's Gorbunov? I've got to open up
his eyes! My God, not one true word . . . I am—
but who am I so self-reproaching of?
To hell with woodsy paranoiacs! Damn!
The warp's gone crazy under which the woof
has lost its thread while sliding home.
It's so peculiar now that Gorchakov
speaks Gorbunov's maniac idiom."

CANTO 5
A Song in the Third Person

"He said to him." "And then he said to him."
"And then he said." "He answered." "And he said."
"Then he." "And he then said into the wind."
"He gazed into the dark and said." "He said
again to him." "But, so to speak, to say
he said is not the same as saying what
he said." "And then he said, 'Don't lose your way
in details; all is clear. That's that.' "
"The one he-said flows on into the next."
"Until he-saids of sin and penance flow
together." "Silent on the table rests
he-said." "And in the end they form a row,
like Tartar yokes." "And then he said to him."
"And he connected his he-said, in line
with that he-said, whose echo echoed thin."
"And then he said to him, and filled the time."

1 4 2

"And then he said." "It is as when a stone
is thrown into a pond. The rings—one, two,
six . . ." "And he said." "The rings are really one,
although the radius is stretched, it's true."
"He-said—a ring." "He-said—another ring."
"And his he-said collided with the ground."
"His own he-said came like a boomerang
back to slap him." "No more new worlds around."
"He said." "He said." "He said." "He said." "He said."
"A train!" "And on a line without an end."
"And starting at the station of He-said."
"And who would want to make the tracks his bed?"
"And then he said." "But in response he said."
"He said, then vanished." "On the platform see
he-said." "He said." "But if he-said's a dead
object, should not the same be true of he?"

"And he to him." "And he." "And he to him."
"All right, let's say the evening has begun."
"And he to him." "And it's no idle whim
to think the two together are but one."
"A question—'he.' " "Whose answer is—'to him.' "
"And vice versa." "Yes, they are the same."
"Though there's a strip of light dividing them."
"Only so that each can have a different name."
"Is he related, then, to him?" "Does not
the world of senseless objects boast of some
relations closed to analytic thought?"
"If not a relative, a sort of chum?"
"What won't the judge's chamber analyze!
The judge sits down; his glasses have no glass."
"Then what is he to him?" "A thin disguise
for the he-said." "That beats in-laws, I guess."

"A massive building. Featureless façade.
Two faces pallid from the stench they breathe."
"They are not here." "And where could they have gone?"
"To the he-said-to-him or to the he."
"A massive building. Through the window peer
two silhouettes." "And pandemonium,

as in a station." "Never silence here?"
"Just in the gaps between he-said-to-him."
"A 'said,' you know, requires she."
"But we've been talking of the said of he."
"But, all in all, the silence pleases me."
"Anathema resounds less threateningly."
"So in this place they're scared of silence?" "No,
they are united by he-said, the way
they are by time and place. It is as though
some grand instinct to incest were at play."

"And that's a form of action, isn't it?"
"Oh yes, for they are full of interplay."
"And will they never quit?" "They'll never quit."
"No doubt it's like a proper noun that way."
"That's right. A proper noun is concentrate.
Substitutions, alterations, slight
omissions—such things cannot enter it."
"And that's the vehicle of questions, right?"
"That's it precisely! Indirect discourse
is in reality the most direct."
"And this is something anyone ignores
at peril of his happiness." "Detect-
ing all pronouncements that he-said recites,
like children by the church doors waiting, one
appears almost to enter in the heights
achieved *before* the dialogue's begun."

"Well, what'd you dream about, He-said-to-him?"
"The doctors are too near." "So what? Go on."
"I dreamed of waves. I dreamed that I could swim
far out to sea." "Unrealistic! Un—"
"Already he's forgotten all about
his mushrooms." "That's impossible!" "Could be."
"He's simply speaking for them both, no doubt."
"That sort of thing absorbs infinity."
"I saw a host of waves pass in review
as clearly as could be. And as they passed
I saw the sky, and just as clearly, too . . ."
"That's something like a double-barreled blast."

". . . the crests, like manes of horses when
they drag a sinking cart, their only thought
is breaking loose." "And weren't there drowning men
or shipwrecks?" "Aivasovsky I am not!
I saw the spuming breakers. And the shore,
a giant horseshoe . . . And, a distance off,
the he-said bustling through the clouds. It wore
the smile of Gorbunov, of Gorchakov."

CANTO 6
Gorbunov and Gorchakov

"Well, what'd you dream of this time, Gorbunov?"
"But I've already told you all about
my meeting with the doctors." "Knock it off.
I overheard it all myself just out
there in the hall." "I'm saying, Gorchakov—"
"That you dream only of the sea, no doubt."
"That's right, the sea." "You are beyond belief."
"I don't insist on your belief. It's not
important." "What a tangled web you weave
with all your lies. It's easy to pick out

a bad egg by its putrid odor! Phew!"
"Just shut your mouth!" "Why should I shut my mouth?"
"Oh, Gorchakov, I know you through and through . . ."
"X-ray technician now?" "Your 'funny' stuff
is out of place, you know. You might live to
regret it." "Oh, imagine that!" "Don't laugh . . .
Why is it the commission always knew
what we'd discussed as soon as you'd gone off?
You played the stoolie for them, didn't you?
So quit your bride-like blushing, Gorchakov."

"You're angry." "I'm not angry." "Don't torment
me, Gorbunov." "I you? That's funny!" "See,
you're angry." "No, I'm not. And if you want,
I'll even swear to God." "But that would be

unpleasant for you." "I'm not hesitant."
"You seemed to say that with sincerity."
"Now you're starting that again? I can't
believe you think it's worth it watching me."
"So then you'll swear to it. I bet you won't
believe me if I do." "Well, probably."

"And *I* don't follow what you mean by that."
"I'm mixing up the chaff and wheat." "You are
unable to believe in anything! No, not
in words, or even holy signs." "There's war
in the Crimea—smoke is all about.
That's something, isn't it? I quote from our
grandfather Krylov . . . Prison's what you've got
ahead, you know." "You ought to go before
they send you." "Hey, what are you gaping at?
"Orlova and Ulanova, two stars."

"I think I'll wander down the hall." "Why?" "Oh,
no reason, just a headache. It's a crime
the way you're always asking questions." "Go
to hell." "What are you after, pal, sublime
illumination?" "Maybe. How 'bout you?"
"You shit! I'm sure you play the stoolie, slime."
"I'm just extending my horizons." "Though
without beliefs." "A skeptic in my prime!
Denunciations, conversations—so
it goes. All helps to brighten up the time."

"And somehow time helps brighten up the days."
"I think my head is better." "So you won't
reveal your dream? Come on, no more delays."
"Oh, all that's sad and ugly. I just want
to watch the lights reflecting on the glass."
"Well, shadows from the boardwalk, friend . . ."
"Ulanova! Orlova, too, who stays
in darkened background!" "Coffee's cold." "They meant
a lot, you know. We were at war, and they
were symbols, of a kind, for our home front."

"The second half of February. Look
at what the hands are pointing to." "It's just
zero's radius." "The numbers?" "Like
the border of a plate . . . I somewhere crossed
this service, *à la* Meissen—" "I relate
to counterfeits." "—*King's Workshop* was embossed
on it, and under that a sun like light
that's beaming from a gasolier." "A glass
of gin right now . . ." "A water bottle I'd
not turn away tonight, if it were passed.

Look there! The shadows stream across the lane!"
"Excuse me, I would rather like to see
us turn the conversation back again . . .
to clocks." "What for?" "You judge more cruelly
than I deserve." "Your own lips are to blame."
"So, is it really zero?" "Yes." "But why?"
"Because outside is emptiness." "But then
inside it's warmer than outside can be."
"But one can simply call a heated room
a product of the freezing earth and sky."

"And what about the woodpiles?" "Well, I guess
they're links between outdoors and in—" "Oh, Lord,
the wind is whistling through the crevices!
I'm freezing cold, and hungry as a bear."
"Physicians aren't as big as sicknesses."
"An inner sanctum's greater than a door."
"It is, you know, a shelter nonetheless."
"Don't be a hypocrite. And furthermore,
remember, Gorchakov: the utterness
of uttered words surpasses disbelief by far."

"Yes, as cold is larger than the heat."
"So, too, the clock hands are inferior
to time." "The hollow in the tree can't beat
the tree." "Though hollows are superior
to squirrels." "Who are certainly more sweet
than eagles." "And the fish . . . that thing . . . so pure . . ."
"I want my body naked, head to feet!"

1 4 7

"Where there's a radius, there's, as it were,
a fork and plate." "And burnt wood—" "Can't compete
with my hot-water bottle, that's for sure."

CANTO 7
Gorbunov and Gorchakov

"Had supper?" "Yeah, a plate of day-old greens.
It's always greens." "We've got the right to eat
bird food here. Still, it's no use making scenes."
"But why do they refuse to give us meat?"
"Look, there's new firewood stacked up between—"
"I have a perfect right to be upset!"
"No, the administration's right. I mean,
it's right within the radius it's set."
"But neither gut nor cranium's too keen
to squeeze inside it." "Let us not repeat

a conversation we've already had . . .
Besides, my kidney's acting up." "But I—
I am outside the radius." "You're mad!
Then who's this standing here?" "A shell, you see."
"When I was young, the soul's infinitude
was something on which one had much to say."
"But me, I'm *married*. Don't you understand?
My wife—and daughter—both outside the ra-
dius." "You need a bracing shower, friend."
"You know one in the neighborhood?" "Well, try

Opochka Station." "Some place you dreamed?" "Like hell!
More likely you dreamed me." "But it's a day
by train out in the provinces!" "You real-
ly get around." "I should escape this." "Why
waste the time and effort? I can tell
you've really put down roots here, anyway."
"You've put down roots here, too." "In general,
I've gotten lazy, though I am, they say,
swift as the wind. It's really not my style
to walk around in hiking boots." "Okay,

1 4 8

calm down." "I'm calm." "How much'd you make?" "A few
hundred, old currency." "Where at?" "A place in . . ."
"Are you thinking I'll report on you?"
"Who would deny himself the fine sensation?"
"*My* silence ain't enough to save you." "True.
Yes, well, you know, on reconsideration . . ."
"You'd rather think me traitor through and through
than try to speculate on a location."
"Alas, my genealogy is too
ignoble to perform such speculation."

"So why attack the menu?" "It's the rut
of eating . . . Well, I'm not a veteran
in here, and this unvaried menu—" "But
you're using restaurants as comparison."
"I'm stretching out the radius somewhat
to get my family in." "They slaughter one
fat lamb a night at home, no doubt." "Well, what
I'm getting at is that it's still too soon
for me to sacrifice the past." "Oh, cut
the crap." "Why call it crap?" "It's overdone."

"I've stretched the radius's distance way
out to my home." "So much the worse, my friend."
"I'm only one leg of the compass. They,
the stationary leg, support me." "And
somehow this helps to brighten up the day,
this wider radius that you command?"
"The narrower. Down here that's just the way
things are: some move as strangers, others stand
still." "Though a stationary lamppost, say,
reflected in a puddle, will expand."

"I'm moving! Look!" "I don't know where the start
is, but I know the end's in Leningrad
snowdrifts." "I move, therefore I am. Descartes
would envy me." "Of course! It makes me glad
to see enthusiasm from the heart."
"As for me, this slumming in your head
is simply boring." "What about your chart:

the Dipper and the skyline, and all that?"
"Aries: it ascends, curating March."
"A telescope's the thing I wish we had."

"Precisely! Then the both of us could see
those fixèd stellar feet." "Progenitors
of motion." "Making the stability
of both Opochka and Kamchatka ours."
"Born late in March, it is my destiny
to wander. I've been fingerprinted . . . stars
are such unstable points of gravity
they set us all to trembling . . ." "Of course,
as one born under Aries, you should be
beneath a cap of Karakulan furs."

"You think I'm trembling from cold?" "That's why
your toes are turning blue." "And you? What is
your sign?" "Well, I belong to Gemini.
Born under Gemini, in May." "I guess
that makes you warm." "I guess." "Come on. Don't try
to play the genius with non-geniuses!"
"Compared to you it's clear enough that I
am scarcely cold at all." "Oh, stop with this!"
"But, Gorchakov, what's wrong?" "It's all a lie!"
"Oh no, it's true—the months and all." "Alas,

we can't afford a telescope. And thus
we'll never see our distant sponsors." "You're
forgetting that, although the radius
is scorned in life, the compass will endure
forever, Gorchakov." "It's hideous—
the possibility of dying here,
believing it's the end." "Ridiculous!
You won't die." "No? You think not?" "Yes." "You're sure?"
"Of course. We cannot carry on into the next
the burden we, in this life, have to bear."

CANTO 8
Gorchakov in the Night

Your line assures me immortality!
My brain, like convolutions in the bed-
clothes—flooded by the glimmer (towering
above my tiny flame) your words have shed.
Colitis is a curse! . . . thoughts clamoring
inside my head like demons in a brood.
Your torch can't seem to set aglow my wick!
Oh, Gorbunov, your words have set my blood
to seething through my cranium, the way
a spark ignites the chips of bone-dry wood.

He's gone . . . He's left me only monologue.
And the night dial's radius . . . He's stored
some apples as security and lobbed
off like Pilate! In the corner curled,
I will inspect the folding of my robe.
I have a salad bowl—I can discard
its dried remains and doff it like a rogue
in a veritable bowler. Where's this starred
empyrean? The ceiling and the rug.
The window—the reflection of the ward.

Night. Windows swirl the ward and double it.
The bulwarks of infinity. They're all
encased in shutters, though, and don't permit
their own reflections farther than the wall.
In that space—rear end forward—one's a bit
uncertain just whose bed is whose. I'd fall
asleep now if I could, though I admit
I'd like to kill myself in general.
And thus—since here a thing's its opposite—
risk delving deeper still into my soul.

I'd like to fall asleep . . . The orderlies
are still on duty . . . Is the room's reflection
helping them? It merely multiplies
the mess . . . Infinity's multiplication.

I watch myself expand before my eyes;
the panes, encouraging imagination,
press a mile into the space that lies
between the bunks. The fiery sensation
gazing at that distant star implies
that gravity is just degeneration.

Regularity in sleep's the core—
indeed, what helps us to recuperate.
So what do I need Gorbunov, then, for?
Whatever for? . . . Shall we abbreviate
our speech by Gorbunov? No gossip's more
explicit than a dream. No eye as great
as dreams. Herr Freud of course has written we're
imprisoned by them . . . Strange to meditate
on this again . . . When there's no other cure,
the grave, of course, will make a hunchback straight . . .

But these disordered musings are the state
that follows from the silence of the near-
by beds. I feel my very self's at stake
when I don't have an interlocutor.
It is in words alone that I partake
of life. They need a witness and an heir!
And, Gorbunov, you are, make no mistake,
my judge. While I am but an agent here,
connecting sleep and sleeplessness, to make
appraisals of front teeth beyond repair.

It's night. The window vent. Oh, if the guard
would only open it! But it's no use.
My face and shoulders are securely barred
in its reflected surface. If the nurse
would open it, a leak would surely start
in the reflection, and, in turn, induce
a wayward patient who was so inspired—
especially since it isn't far—to loose
his face at least en route to Leningrad.

Oh, Gorbunov! Like any simpleton,
I feel I'm nothing but the radius
a clock hand makes! To wait for me—beyond
the bordered plate or here—I'd have to guess
pitifully, there isn't anyone.
For these dimensions are, for you, alas
too circumscribed. Ahead your martyrdom
is waiting: it's been fitted to your size.
The horror there's a variation on
a ladder's rung, a little door, the pass

where you're expected for too long. My sin
is only that my call won't get to you.
You, Gorbunov! As long as I am in
this world, I know I must surrender to
your power! To you I raise my prayers. I can
go nowhere that your words do not pursue
me. Come to me, I beg you, speak again!
I have to hear your words resounding through
the air. If I've denounced them, it has only been
because I cannot part with them, I know.

Forgive me when you leave me here at last.
It isn't that I fear our parting when,
with walking papers crumpled in my fist,
I finally stretch to you my parting hand.
Like all one has to bear—the catalyst
of boredom and indifference—my friend,
do not resent me, crave revenge. At best
I'm like an echo which continues sound
to save it, in the end, from being lost:
I love you and betray you, too, to pain."

CANTO 9

Gorbunov and the Doctors

"Well, Gorbunov, we've brought you here to tell
us everything." "About?" "Your dreams." "About
the compass." "And your daughter." "And the shell."

"And give us names, details." "Let's see. I doubt
my daughter figures in my dreams at all.
In fact, I'm sure of it." "Oh, cut it out!"
"Come on!" "I dreamed about the sea." "Oh hell!"
"Let's do without the wet stuff." "And without
'anchors aweigh' and 'o'er the seas' as well."
"About Opochka . . ." "Can't imagine what

you're after that one for." "For your own good."
"A line that smacks—" "It's necessary. We—"
"—that smacks of questions that Red Riding Hood
asked Granny. You'll recall, I'm sure, that she
inquired about the ears . . . 'Don't be afraid . . .'
She answers, 'Oh, I am afraid . . .' 'Tee-hee—
the better, pet, to hear you with.' " "Who would
have figured that he would turn out to be
a coward." "Anyway, the girl is saved."
"There is a plus in everything, you see."

"Say something, Gorbunov." "You realize
that we'll get angry if you make us wait
too long." "What are you waiting for?" "For lies
unmet by protests to evaporate."
"And then?" "Well, then I think it would be nice
to speak on equal terms, don't you?" "I hate
his whimpering, his stupid shrugs and sighs.
Nurse, an injection will facilitate . . ."
"He's trembling." "Naturally. The needle's size
has caused his thinking to accelerate."

"Well, Gorbunov, recalled your dream?" "It was
the sea. Just that." "No chanterelles?" "In short,
alas, there are no more of them." "Alas?"
"A habit. I got used to their support."
"It often happens, when their women pass
away or go away, that men resort
to words of grief like that." " 'Alas'—a man's
word, when it's said in quotes." "But it's the sort
of word one's likely to hear widows use."
"We'll put that down as well in the report."

"Dreams bare the secret canvas of a man,
of what takes place inside." "And what the eyes
observe is of less interest to us than
what's hidden, for the reason that—" "What lies
outside is Gorchakov. I know." "Well then,
the point is not the mischievous disguise
he has assumed; it's what your dreams make plain:
you gravitate to darker depths." "I guess
I'm dreaming like the Neva flows, you mean.
But mouths of rivers speak not of demise,

but just the opposite: of procreation."
"It's scarcely bearable that any freak
or bum should dump descendants on the nation."
"A pity. For the river, as the Greek
philosopher remarked, though flowing, stays in
one place." "Which is the problem all men seek
to solve." "And Newton's moral." "There! He's raising
Newton!" "And Lomonosov." "Outside?" "A week
in February. Time of hibernation,
denunciations, snowstorms." "It's unique

among the months, in terms of days." "A kind
of cripple." "Don't you think it easier
to live through?" "Shamefully. In fact, I find
it easier than easy to endure."
"And rivers?" "What about them?" "Don't they bind
themselves in ice?" "But it was man we were—"
"Know what awaits you?" "I suspect a signed
certificate committing me." "Yes, sir.
Considering the things you have in mind,
We'll have to keep you on forever here."

"What for? . . . However, well, it's obvious
one must control oneself to be let go."
"And call for Gorchakov." "One can discuss
the stars with him." "Of course." "Which goes to show
that there's a plus in most things." "Yes, a plus!"
"And he, like God, is omnipresent, though
he's in the habit of denouncing us."

1 5 5

"It's nails that hold a horseshoe up, you know."
"How strange that Gorbunov, nailed to the cross,
must look for help from Gorchakov below."

"But why exaggerate like this? Why mumble
these Golgothan thoughts?" "But can't you see
that this is a catastrophe." "You bundle
eternity up with catastrophe."
"Eternity's the bung that plugs the bunghole.
That's why he doesn't want eternity."
"Yes, this is all too hard for him to follow."
"Hey, Gorbunov, you want a cup of tea?"
"Oh, why have you forsaken me?" "Dear fellow,
whom are you calling now?" "He seems to be

lamenting Gorchakov again." "Why not
his daughter or his wife? Why Gorchakov?"
"The whole thing's egotism." "You sure we've got
it right? It's really Gor—" "Hey, Gorbunov!
Look here, your fate has been decided." "What
of Gorchakov's?" "Well, live with the rebuff:
we're freeing him. You're on your own. I'd not
waste sighs on such a creep." "From this day forth,
as usual, my friend, when life is shot,
eternity begins." "Speech signing off."

CANTO 10
A Conversation on the Porch

"A massive city in its twilight shroud."
"The streets, like lines in ledgers, parallel."
"A massive madhouse stands." "Looks like a void
existing at the center of the well-
planned universe." "The gate obscures from view
an icy courtyard filled with snow and cords
of wood." "Which is a conversation, too,
since all these things have been described in words."
"Out here are men, and there, the lunatics
who know internal and eternal pain."

1 5 6

"Not 'men' themselves?" "But can one ever fix
the title to one's neighbor?" "They're not men?
The expressions in the eyes, the stance, the frame:
head, sturdy shoulders, legs, and arms that reach . . ."
"The moment that we give a thing a name,
that thing's transformed into a part of speech."
"But what about the body?" "It obeys
the rule." "And what about this place?" "It's called
a madhouse." "And the days?" "Their names are days."
"Oh, everything's transformed again to old

Gomorrah, built of greedy words. But how
do they come by the right?" "—A word that rings
a nasty bell." "My head's already so
besotted with these words devouring things."
"No question that it causes heads to spin."
"As seas make Gorbunov's; it's for the birds."
"And so it's not the sea that surges in-
to shore, but words are overlapping words."
"And words are sort of holy relics." "Yes,
though once things hung . . . Names are defense
against the very things that they express."
"Against the sense of life?" "Well, in a sense."
"Do they defend against the Passion, too?"
"Against all passions." "God forbid!" "For He
designed His lips for words . . . But then He drew
forth words in His defense." "Well, basically,
that's why His life is so prophetic. It's
insurance that we won't go down, but swim."
"And thus His life's the one thing that admits
two meanings." "It's, therefore, a synonym."

"But what about eternity? Does it
resemble He-said in a Cossack coat?"
"It is the only word that hasn't yet
devoured its earthly object in its throat."
"A hardy word-shield!" "Hardly." "Yet the man
protected by the cross is saved, at least."
"Not fully so." "You mean the synonym
can give no greater guarantee than this?"

"That's true." "But what of love? Can love not stem
the tide of aimless chatter?" "Either you've
descended from the sphere of seraphim
or you're confusing potency with love."
"No word is so devoid of telltale signs."
"And there's no cover that has so devoured
its object, obfuscating its designs.
And nothing is so rending as a word."
"But try regarding this objectively;
to wit: the general observation seems
to be that words are also things, so we
are saved at last!" "It's then the silence comes.

Silence is the future of the days
that roll toward speech, with all we emphasize
in it, as, in our greetings, silence pays
respect to unavoidable goodbyes.
Silence is the future of the words
whose vowels have gobbled up internally
the stuff of things, things with a terror towards
their corners; a wave that cloaks eternity.
Silence is the future of our love;
a space, not an impediment, a space
depriving love's blood-throbbed falsetto of
its echo, of its natural response.
Silence is the present for the men
who lived before us. And, procuress-like,
silence gathers all together in
itself, admitted by the speech-filled present. Life
is but a conversation in the face
of silence." "Gestures, quarrels, men incensed."
"A twilight talking to a murky close."
"With walls that stand like arguments against."

"A massive city in its twilight shroud."
"A speech by chaos, rendered plain as hell."
"Here stands the massive madhouse, like a void
existing at the center of the well-
planned universe." "Goddamn this draft!" "Your curse
won't hurt my ears. My friend, it isn't life

1 5 8

before me but a victory of words."
"And verily the nouns are verbalized!"
"A bird flies upward from its nest when food
is what the little bird is looking for."
"Indeed, a star that climbs above the field
seeks out a brighter interlocutor."
"And all night long, as far as one can view,
with postal slowness, in its turn, the plain
keeps up the conversation." "How can it, too?"
"By means of jaggedness in the terrain."
"But can one, at such distance, hear enough
to know which blabbermouth he bothers with?"
"The higher pitch belongs to Gorbunov,
to Gorchakov, the low." "For what it's worth."

CANTO 11
Gorbunov and Gorchakov

"So, what'd you dream of this time?" "Nothing new."
"Then I won't ask." "What's this? You feeling racked
by shame or something suddenly?" "No, view
it simply as a sense of measure, tact."
"How very generous." "What can I do?
This place has gotten to me. And the fact—"
"What fact?" "That I have landed here." "Oh, you
are capable of causing cardiac
arrest. Just take your facts and go to . . . to . . ."
"Come off it now. We've got to interact."

"And who am I to you?" "I wouldn't know."
"No matter . . . So I guess you're leaving. When?"
"Right after Easter." "And from here you'll go . . . ?"
"Home." "They won't hesitate to take you in?"
"They won't." "Where do you live?" "The address? Oh,
I never give that out to anyone."
"That strikes me as a lie." "If you say so."
"Don't tell me fairy tales." "But then again
you won't be coming by to visit." "No?
And why is that?" "Because the outcome's been

decided." "Then you're right." "I think I am."
"You *think* so?" "Oh, I'm sorry! That popped out
by accident. I've no right to dream
of doubt." "So tell me, when you're home, about
the house, how d'you think you'll pass the time?"
"That's my concern." "You're the one who thought
that we should 'interact.' And yet your tone
is hardly conversational. It's odd."
"It's just my nature." "Well, an apple, then,
to change your mood?" "Okay, a nibble, but
I promise I won't take the goods and run . . .

'Lift 'n' heave'—that's my kind of work. Believe
me, pal, all others are superfluous."
"My eyes are being shrouded! Lift 'n' heave,
take 'er away—oh, that's synonymous
with all that happens to me now." "Be brave.
We promise not to drop you." " '*We?*' What does
'we' mean?" "Don't be afraid. Before I leave
I'll teach you palmistry." "If that's the case
I turn my back on you." "You mean that we've
no friendship left? There's no more to discuss?

You could be kinder." "Evidently this
is what my genes designed." "Existence, though,
determines—" "Tea?" "Okay . . . deter—" "I guess
it's cold. You want it warmed a bit?" "Uh, no . . .
cold's fine . . . determines consciousness."
"I'd take that sentence left to right." "Ah, so
you think I am a Jew?" "This apple was
plucked from the tree of knowledge by a Jew."
"No, it was Eve who did the plucking, ass."
"Eve may have, but it seems he did it, too."

"But still, he was a genius in his way.
He founded science, and he's got a name
that's sonorous, in any case." "Let's try
to skip the names. That palindrome
would set them chopping off my hands today."
"You know, he, too, consigned himself to pain.

And now he has whole peoples in his sway."
"Panmongolism! There's a loaded term."
"He was condemned as well." "You mean to say
he was condemned to parting?" "Just condemned."

"But what is parting?" "Must we linger on
this word?" "It's for my files. Elucidate
the ways of parting." "They depend upon
from whom one parts. That's what's at stake.
Where you remain. Can you remain as one,
named So-and-so, in such a place and state?
And if from someone close, to whom he's gone
and for how long." "And if forever?" "Wait . . .
You stand and gape into the dark, alone—
the sort of dark that lowered lids create

for sleeping in. And so you shudder now
and then from grief. The darkness, being real,
is clearly visible. Though now, you know,
there isn't any sea or chanterelle."
"And even in the spring you think it's so?
The springtime makes it easier, I feel."
"I doubt it." "—doubt it gazing at the snow."
"You're like a thing extracted from a field."
"Unlike a gum, the earth's not bleeding, though."
"This evidently is as God has willed.

And what does parting mean to you?" "Decay . . .
Doors closed behind you as you disappear.
And, if it's day, the brilliance of the day."
"And if it's night?" "At night the atmosphere
comes into play—perhaps a single stray
light or a bench in some deserted square."
"And does the memory of a loved one stay
with you for long?" "You'd better be more clear."
"Well, after losing me what will you say?"
"In general, loss isn't hard to bear."

"If that's the way you feel about it, why
go on about our 'friendship'?" "In this instance

1 6 1

we're the better for the fact that we
live here together at this little distance:
the reason being that to really be—"
" 'Really to be'! Or, better yet, 'existence' . . ."
"—to really cease to be . . . Nonentity
will make my absence give, for one who listens
to the plain, it's plain monotony."
"You mean, therefore, that you will be my silence."

CANTO 12
Gorbunov and Gorchakov

"Have you had supper?" "Have indeed. And you?"
"Uh-huh." "How'd you like the cabbage mush?"
"In texture, cabbage mush gives little to
the palate; and it didn't fill me much."
"It's watery and empty as a rule—
so quoth the proverb." "Sad." "Could use a dash
of vinegar, for pungency, it's true."
"Well, all is empty." "But one emptiness
tastes different from another one." "I do
yearn for a thing to sink my teeth in, yes."

"In this hell-hole into which we're cast,
there's nothing left to do but to begin
a month before the start of Lent to fast."
"I guess you're speaking of the madhouse, then."
"Our geography is small, at best."
"And afterwards?" "You're always asking! When
is afterwards?" "When crucifixion's past."
"And what's that mean?" "It's just an idiom."
"You'd think they'd use some basil leaves at least."
"As usual they'd mix the bromide in."

"Yeah, none of this will turn out well, I fear.
This bromide is unhealthy, nasty stuff."
"It's dispossessing all of us of hair.
Just look at any pillow: daily fluff
is sacrificed by our Babanov there,

Mickiewicz sheds his eyebrows, and I have
now lost the battle on my crown. I swear
the dope makes you anemic." "Cools you off
between the devil and the rib—that's where
it sits, so we don't wreck our brains with love."

"I took it in the army." "You alone?"
"No, everyone. We called it 'Unmanalov' or
'Antihardon,' 'cause with just a dram
we all forgot Ulanova-Orlova."
"Mine was dark, but now it's gone so blond!
The warp is gone on which this rug was woven.
It won't make the gray it would have gone . . ."
"But don't forget the basic circumstances given."
"And what, dear sir, is that supposed to mean?"
"That you won't need it at the rate you're going."

"You're right." "Don't shake." "I'm cold." "Here, put your hands
beneath the blanket." "Thank you. Tell me, what
is love?" "I told you . . ." "But I know that sounds
each bear their various boundaries; they've got
many different levels." "Love still stands
for parting's preface." "No!" "I'm willing that
I be a monument to lies, who sends
his children and their progeny to fart
upon his head!" "Come on, don't be a dunce.
I said that 'cause, as usual, I'm bored."

"Damn the draft in here! It chills the blood!"
"They've puttied shut the cracks." "Now there's a joke.
The radiator's cold as well." "It's cold
and dirty in this place around the clock."
"There's a star above that tree I could
discern without a telescope." "You look
at one; no star ascends without a brood."
"It's just occurred to me, just as a lark:
what if they chopped the cross for firewood—
would its image rise again in smoke?"

"You're nuts." "I'm only showing some concern
for your affairs." "Praiseworthy charity!
What are you really after, though?" "The churn
of warmth back in a cold extremity."
"You said it. Mine are all about to turn
to ice." "I'm right." "There's inhumanity
in that." "Let's lay the logs star-shaped to burn."
"You're right. Stars bring to mind eternity—
unlike the cross, I am ashamed to own."
"I'd rather say a bad infinity."

"What time is it?" "Apparently it's night."
"Oh, please, don't start in on the zodiac."
"I know my wife and daughter are outside."
"Well, what I said of love is as exact
for marriage." "For myself, I wouldn't mind
it someday. But for you it's a mistake."
"My marriage irritates you, I've divined."
"You should have wed the darkness." "I can't hack
monotony. Indeed, I take delight
in each domestic jam and cul-de-sac."

"What time is it? It's almost zero." "Oh.
That late." "Since I have no mathematic prowess,
I'll tell you I consider every 0
a forerunner of plus." "My lips, empowered
by yawning and by biting, quickly go
to circle." "What's achieved, then, when you throw it
all into a single heap?" "The snow-
capped pinnacles where unscaled Elbrus towered."
"Did earth create concavity that's so
immense?" "It showed itself to be a coward."

"If mountains are to be your leitmotif,
then think about Golgotha; March 15,
the Ides of March, is almost here, and I've
made up my mind to jump in some ravine."
"Or wrap yourself up in a cloud, as if
in some black Persian veil. And in that scene
you'll play the spirit." "Well, you measure with

a yardstick of your own. However, mine
won't measure that two-headed summit. It
just presses all the courtyard snowdrifts down."

CANTO 13
Conversations about the Sea

"One is immortal, goes your argument.
But to the sorrow of your prophecy,
I am already half an invalid.
Your light cannot drive off the dark from me—
not any more than night-lights by the bed
drive off my dreams. I don't reproach you. We
must stop reproach. Isn't that the point?
Before my open or my shutting eye
something mighty always seethes ahead
as if it were the sea. I think it is the sea.

It's night. The hospital. On hostile ground.
I cannot bear to listen to you lest
I tremble from the cold and shame about
that torch. Because the sea will never best
its own concavity. I won't go down
into it, though. Though truth is dearer . . . Trust
I won't allow you into any harm!
Enough of that! It seems you hardly rest
in certainty that it's the sea around
us and not simply . . . woe. Oh, *why* this test?"

"Perhaps it is indeed the sea . . . the cries
of gulls above a woman tossing crumbs
of bread from off a pier. And like the waves
her flounce flaps in the wind; her ragged hem
is slapping at her shoes. So, in a blaze
of screeching battle, there she stands alone:
she tosses bread and stares into the haze . . .
As if, become farsighted for a time,
she holds a bee in Turkey in her gaze."

"Yeah, that's the sea. Precisely that. The deep
of life from which, like knights in chain-mail coats,
so very long ago we all sprang up
that if you hadn't struck this distant note
again just now, I would have let it sleep,
forgetting that, in fact, the world has got
a bottom and horizon and a type
of space besides this one where it's our fate
to stare at painted walls, a lilac stripe.
But 'he that hath ears to hear, let him be mute.' "

"There's something bigger in the world than us,
a thing that warms us, though it doesn't warm
itself; that, with the help of Boreas,
stuffs hollows up with hills, collecting them
around to be of one another's use.
I feel as though I'm striding through a dream:
upstairs to light, downstairs to the abyss,
up to the threshold of Elysium,
all by myself, amid the blooming crests
where Nereus' escalators hum."

"But ocean's a too-foreign element
to buy the story of some 'Tally ho'
across it. Ice of course is different.
No, Gorbunov, the end of all your woe
is not in sight. It seems that you are meant
to measure out your grief in years—you know,
just like they did in Exodus. I can't
say where each year your wanderings will go,
where water's woven into sky . . . this tent
of sky's so broad, for whom can one man howl?"

"My soul's too weak for calling. From now on,
wherever fate sees fit for me to be,
from Paradise to squatting in the john,
not painted walls but waves are what I'll see.
And that's not bragging, Gorchakov. A man
like me, in such celestial disarray,
well, what would he be pleading for? For one

who hath the ears to hear, artillery
repeat of waves is far more pleasant than
a tearful prayer that this cup pass from me."

"But that's a sin! . . . What's wrong with me? Today
I, cursing you, forgot that woodpile scene's
details: you asked about (as I replay
it in my head) my dreams. And in response
I tried to speak my mind, that dreams employ
the heritage of day. And then it seems
you called my mushrooms islands. I reply:
How hard it is beneath our craniums!
And now you see the sea—to that I say,
Absurd! Though yours has greater rights, the dreams

are both the same." "And sleep?" "The doctors' cure:
the core of cores." "And like in streams, we sink
in it." "We sink into the darkness. Your
imagination sucks. What cripple-think!"
"Sleep's an exit from the blackness." "Gor-
bunov forgets the age we're trapped within.
I tell you that your dream's not new!" "But nor
is man." "Why speak of man?" " 'Cause man's a thing
that dreams alone can take the credit for."
"And what about a man is most distinct?"

"The eyelids. Close them, you see darkness, right?"
"But in the light?" "In light, too, as a rule . . .
And suddenly you see, your eyes shut tight,
a feature. One, a second . . . third . . . You feel
your ears hum; your mouth's cold. The height
of sky. And children running down the quay. A gull
is catching bread crumbs midway through its flight."
"Am I not there? On that embankment?" "All
I see, that moment, everything in sight
is real—more real than you there on your stool."

CANTO 14
Conversation in a Conversation

"But that's delirium! You hear? So look,
we need a witness . . . Here, Babanov, you.
Now, in a robe without a belt or hook,
I'll perch upon this stool in public view.
Well, Gorbunov, you see me, right?" "I took
no notice." "Even of my long johns' hue?"
"No." "I'll obliterate your portrait! Look
here, Gorbunov! The sea becomes a stew
now that the wind is kicking up! You snake,
you hear?" "I have already answered no."

"So that's the way it is! Well then, let's use
our fists! Taught! Blockheads must be taught a lesson!
Take that! Well now, can you conjecture whose
hand hit you—mine? Babanov's?" "In that session?
um, well, was it . . . Gor-banov's?" "You refuse
to blame me! You'd forgive my sins! Your ocean
will burst the faucets soon, and you'll know whose!"
"He-he." "What are you laughing at, you crashing
idiot! You fool!" "Hey, what's the noise?"
"Get out of here, Mickiewicz!" "I'm the boss in

here, and if a pal has closed his eyes,
the more so as it's night already, those
around him should, I think, shut up." "You flies!
I slugged him, well, because . . . he didn't close
his eyes from pain." "I really do advise
you to shut up." "Mickiewicz, your brain loose
or what? What's wrong with you? It isn't wise,
you know, opposing me." "I'll bust your nose!"
"Ouch, ouch, my corns!" "What's going on, you guys?"
"Damned if I know." "Someone got his toes

stepped on." "Watch it, I hear the doctors!" "Jeez-
us Christ! Get in the sack, quick!" "I'm in bed."
"And, Gorbunov, don't you so much as sneeze.
Just cover up and . . ." "But he's really dead

1 6 8

asleep already." "What?" "I hear the keys!"
"Asleep? Impossible! You're cracked!" "I said
shut up, you fool!" "Babanov, don't you tease."
"Leave him alone." "I only want a bit . . ."
"Just you try squealing, Gorbunov." "But he's
asleep." "Oh no. We're really in for it."

"How should you greet your doctors?" "Showing some
respect . . . Get up, you crippled lunatics!"
"You got a gripe about the grub, you scum?"
"There was a fight in here. I heard it." "Nix,
my friend, there wasn't." "Don't be quarrelsome.
The night clerk said he heard a fight." "I'll fix
that liar!" "Save your tricks. We're not so dumb."
"Whose stream is that?" "Some dick's." "Who mentioned dicks?
I asked you whose it is, not where it's from."
"Yes, whose? An eagle's?" "Yours, you Cossack pricks."

"Mickiewicz!" "Yeah?" "Well, wipe it up, you creep!"
"We keep the peace here. Better learn your place."
"What's wrong with Gorbunov?" "Uh . . . he's asleep."
"So get to sleep and don't disturb the peace."
"We're on our way." "That's right. Bad little sheep."
"We're going." "We'll hear houseflies buzz
you'll be so quiet. Got it? Not a peep!"
"Excuse me, fellows, but I've got to piss."
"Tomorrow." "Gorchakov, they're in your keep."
"Here's news for you: a sputnik is in space."

"They've gone." "Hey, Gorchakov! What's that? Your piss?"
"Go f——." "All right, let's close our little eyes."
"I'd love to have a cake for Easter." "Yes,
to break the fast. Some butter, some good-size
salami . . ." "You should have asked the doctor." "Guess
you could've—he was asking, doctor-wise."
"In the confusion I forgot." "I wish
you'd shut . . ." "Hey, look at Gorchakov, you guys!
He's whispering to Gorbunov, his lips
pressed close." "He's trying to apologize."

"You're really sleeping? Far as I can tell,
you're really sleeping . . . how the strands are wound
in knots! I cannot understand myself . . .
For God's sake, please forgive, forgive me, friend.
Here, let me fluff this battered pillow full.
How's that? . . . my self and self are out of tune.
Forgive me . . . This is more than I can well
perform. Now, sleep . . . to speak of glances, one
could not find much to pause on here, where all
is obstacle. On obstacles alone.

Sleep, Gorbunov. Until they sound
retreat. I only want to guard your rest.
To hell with it! with the alarum's round!
Though obstacles are new to you, I'm used
to them. Forgive me for my bragging, friend.
Forgive me my disharmony, at best.
Sleep, sleep, and I will wait beside your bed.
Not over you, not under, but here next
to you . . . Don't care how many years they send
you up! I'll wait to meet your opened eyes.

What do you see? The sea? Two seas or more?
You wander wave-filled hallways . . . Fishes stare
with dumb expressions out of every door.
I'm right behind you . . . But from God knows where
ten thousand bubbles bubble up before
my eyes . . . And I can't follow, I can't bear
the pressure . . . What? What's that? My mind's gone . . . or
hallucinating conversation . . . Look there!
Down from the north the wind's begun to roar!
The pillow's squashed, the part has left your hair."

[*1968 / Translated by Harry Thomas*]

170

Notes

To a Friend: In Memoriam / *Natalia Goncharova (1812–63):* Pushkin's wife.

Lithuanian Nocturne / III. *Zhemaitija:* Lithuanian name for Samogitia, a historical region of western Lithuania. / IV. *Stasis Girenas (1893–1933)* and *Steponas Darius (1896–1933):* American aviators of Lithuanian origin, who crashed near Soldin, Lithuania, after successfully flying across the Atlantic. They were widely believed to have been shot down by the Nazis. / XII. *Prince Vytautus (c. 1350–1430):* Grand prince and most famous monarch of early Lithuania. / XXI. *St. Casimir (d. 1484):* Patron saint of Lithuania. *St. Nicholas (d. 324):* Patron saint of Russia.

Twenty Sonnets to Mary Queen of Scots / I. *"all the dead past now lives anew in my cold heart."* From a popular nineteenth-century Russian love song. / II. *Zarah Leander:* Swedish actress and singer popular in the 1940s. She played Mary, Queen of Scots, in the German film *Das Herz einer Königin.* / VI. *Parmenides:* Greek philosopher of the Eleatic School, c. 515 B.C. / X. *crippled Hamburg cooper:* From Gogol's *Diary of a Madman.*

Minefield Revisited / *Sophia Kovalevska (1850–91):* A celebrated mathematician.

Eclogue IV: Winter / VII. *Terek:* A river in the Caucasus. / IX. *Kazimir Malevich (1878–1935):* Russian suprematist painter.

Eclogue V: Summer / I. *"cock and hen":* A children's guessing game played with meadow grass. *Terzaromaville:* Moscow is traditionally identified as the "Third Rome." / IV. *Simonides (556–468 B.C.?):* Greek lyric poet.

Kellomäki / XI. *Nikolai Lobachevsky (1793–1856):* Mathematician who proposed the theory that parallel lines converge in infinity.

The Fly / VI. *"six-legged letters":* The Cyrillic letter Ж indicates the *zh* sound.

Afterword / *Kuzbas:* Acronym for an industrial region in Siberia.

Gorbunov and Gorchakov / Gorbunov (from the Russian *gorbun,* "hunched") and Gorchakov (from *gor'kii,* "bitter") are patients in a "psychiatric hospital" on the outskirts of Leningrad. / I. *dreams:* The Russian *son* means both "sleep" and "dream." *The Crosses:* A prison in Leningrad. / V. *Ivan Aivazovsky (1817–1900):* Seascape painter. / VI. *Ivan Krylov (1768–1844):* Satirist and poet, famous for his fables. *Lyubov Orlova (1902–75):* Film star. *Galina Ulanova (b. 1910):* Dancer with the Bolshoi Ballet. / IX. *Mikhail Lomonosov*

(1711–65): Russian scientist, scholar, poet. / XI. *Panmongolism, say. How much there is to that:* Parody of Soloviev's epigraph to Blok's poem "The Scythians." / XII. *Elbrus:* Highest peak in the Caucasus. / XIII. *like knights in chain-mail coats:* From Pushkin's *Tale of Tsar Saltan.*

READ MORE IN PENGUIN

Penguin Twentieth-Century Classics offer a selection of the finest works of literature published this century. Spanning the globe from Argentina to America, from France to India, the masters of prose and poetry are represented by the Penguin.

If you would like a catalogue of the Twentieth-Century Classics library, please write to:

Penguin Marketing, 27 Wrights Lane, London W8 5TZ

(Available while stocks last)

READ MORE IN PENGUIN

A CHOICE OF TWENTIETH-CENTURY CLASSICS

Ulysses James Joyce

Ulysses is unquestionably one of the supreme masterpieces, in any artistic form, of the twentieth century. 'It is the book to which we are all indebted and from which none of us can escape' – T. S. Eliot

The Heart of the Matter Graham Greene

Scobie is a highly principled police officer in a war-torn West African state. When he is passed over for promotion he is forced to borrow money to send his despairing wife on holiday. With a duty to repay his debts and an inability to distinguish between love, pity and responsibility to others and to God, Scobie moves inexorably towards his final damnation.

The Age of Innocence Edith Wharton

To the rigid world of propriety, of which Old New York is composed, returns the Countess Olenska. Separated from her European husband and displaying an independence and impulsive awareness of life, she stirs the educated sensitivity of Newland Archer, who is engaged to be married to young May Welland.

Mr Noon D. H. Lawrence

This Penguin edition is the first annotated paperback publication of Lawrence's autobiographical and strikingly innovative unfinished novel. Abandoning a promising academic career, Gilbert Noon becomes embroiled in an affair which causes him to flee to Germany, there to find true passion with the unhappily married wife of an English doctor.

Black List, Section H Francis Stuart

This astonishingly powerful novel follows H on a spiritual quest for revelation and redemption, from his disastrous marriage to Iseult Gonne, the Irish Civil War and internment, to his life as a writer, poultry farmer, racehorse owner and Bohemian in 1930s London, and his arrival in Hitler's Germany in 1940.

READ MORE IN PENGUIN

A CHOICE OF TWENTIETH-CENTURY CLASSICS

Orlando   Virginia Woolf

Sliding in and out of three centuries, and slipping between genders, Orlando is the sparkling incarnation of the personality of Vita Sackville-West as Virginia Woolf saw it.

Selected Poems   Patrick Kavanagh

One of the major figures in the modern Irish poetic canon, Patrick Kavanagh (1904–67) was a post-colonial poet who released Anglo-Irish verse from its prolonged obsession with history, ethnicity and national politics. His poetry, written in an uninhibited vernacular style, focused on the 'common and banal' aspects of contemporary life.

More Die of Heartbreak   Saul Bellow

'One turns the last pages of *More Die of Heartbreak* feeling that no image has been left unexplored by a mind not only at constant work but standing outside itself, mercilessly examining the workings, tracking the leading issues of our times and the composite man in an age of hybrids' – *New York Book Review*

Tell Me How Long the Train's Been Gone   James Baldwin

Leo Proudhammer, a successful Broadway actor, is recovering from a near-fatal heart attack. Talent, luck and ambition have brought him a long way from the Harlem ghetto of his childhood. With Barbara, a white woman who has the courage to love the wrong man, and Christopher, a charismatic black revolutionary, Leo faces a turning-point in his life.

Memories of a Catholic Girlhood   Mary McCarthy

Blending memories and family myths, Mary McCarthy takes us back to the twenties, when she was orphaned in a world of relations as colourful, potent and mysterious as the Catholic religion. 'Superb ... so heartbreaking that in comparison Jane Eyre seems to have got off lightly' – Anita Brookner

READ MORE IN PENGUIN

A CHOICE OF TWENTIETH-CENTURY CLASSICS

The Complete Saki Saki

Macabre, acid and very funny, Saki's work drives a knife into the upper crust of English Edwardian life. Here are the effete and dashing heroes, Reginald, Clovis and Comus Bassington, and tea on the lawn with articulate duchesses, the smell of gunshot and the tinkle of the caviar fork, and here is the half-seen, half-felt menace of disturbing undercurrents . . .

Nineteen Eighty-Four George Orwell

'It is a volley against the authoritarian in every personality, a polemic against every orthodoxy, an anarchistic blast against every unquestioning conformist . . . *Nineteen Eighty-Four* is a great novel and a great tract because of the clarity of its call, and it will endure because its message is a permanent one: erroneous thought is the stuff of freedom' – Ben Pimlott

The Levant Trilogy Olivia Manning

Leaving behind Hitler's Europe, Guy and Harriet Pringle find refuge in Cairo, a city tense with fear and expectation. 'Her lucid and unsentimental style conveys the full force of ordinary reality with its small betrayals and frustrations but, at the back of it, images of another and more enduring life emerge' – *The Times*

A First Omnibus Ivy Compton-Burnett
A Family and a Fortune • Parents and Children • A God and His Gifts

'Ivy Compton-Burnett is one of the most original, artful and elegant writers of our century . . . She invented her own way of writing a novel; form and content (unlike her characters) make the happiest of marriages' – Hilary Mantel

Selected Short Stories Rabindranath Tagore

Rabindranath Tagore (1861–1941) was the grand master of Bengali culture, and in the 1890s he concentrated on creating a new form, the short story. His work has been acclaimed for its vivid portrayal of Bengali life and landscapes, brilliantly polemical in its depiction of peasantry and gentry, the caste system, corrupt officialdom and dehumanizing poverty.

READ MORE IN PENGUIN

A CHOICE OF TWENTIETH-CENTURY CLASSICS

Flight to Arras   Antoine de Saint-Exupéry

On 22 May 1940 Antoine de Saint-Exupéry set off on a reconnaissance operation from Orly over Nazi-occupied France to Arras. It was such a dangerous mission that he was not expected to survive it. *Flight to Arras* is his profound and passionate meditation on mortality and war, on his wretched, defeated country and the seeds of its regeneration.

Mrs Dalloway   Virginia Woolf

Into *Mrs Dalloway* Virginia Woolf poured all her passionate sense of how other people live, remember and love as well as hate, and in prose of astonishing beauty she struggled to catch, impression by impression and minute by minute, the feel of life itself.

The Counterfeiters   André Gide

'It's only after our death that we shall really be able to hear.' From puberty through adolescence to death, *The Counterfeiters* is a rare encyclopedia of human disorder, weakness and despair.

A House for Mr Biswas   V. S. Naipaul

'*A House for Mr Biswas* can be seen as the struggle of a man not naturally rebellious, but in whom rebellion is inspired by the forces of ritual, myth and custom ... It has the Dickensian largeness and luxuriance without any of the Dickensian sentimentality, apostrophizing or preaching' – Paul Theroux

Talkative Man   R. K. Narayan

Bizarre happenings at Malgudi are heralded by the arrival of a stranger on the Delhi train who takes up residence in the station waiting-room and, to the dismay of the station master, will not leave. 'His lean, matter-of-fact prose has lost none of its chuckling sparkle mixed with melancholy' – *Spectator*

READ MORE IN PENGUIN

A CHOICE OF TWENTIETH-CENTURY CLASSICS

The Golden Bough James Frazer

James George Frazer (1854–1941) caught the popular imagination with his vast and enterprising comparative study of the beliefs and institutions of mankind. This edition is Frazer's own single-volume abridgement of 1922.

The Slave Isaac Bashevis Singer

'*The Slave* – the finest, most lyrical of his novels – is replete with the sounds and smells of the Polish countryside ... the best of his writing warms the heart and reaffirms one's beleaguered faith in pitiful humanity' – Paul Bailey

The Quiet American Graham Greene

The Quiet American is a terrifying portrait of innocence at large. While the French Army in Indo-China is grappling with the Vietminh, back at Saigon a young and high-minded American begins to channel economic aid to a 'Third Force'. 'There has been no novel of any political scope about Vietnam since Graham Greene wrote *The Quiet American*' – *Harper's*

Letters 1931–1966 Jean Rhys

The publication of *Wide Sargasso Sea* finally brought Jean Rhys to fame at the age of seventy-six. These letters span the period of the completion of her masterpiece and make exhilarating as well as painful reading, providing a frank self-portrait of a fascinating, complex, tormented personality striving to know herself.

The Desert of Love François Mauriac

Two men, father and son, share a passion for the same woman. Maria Cross is attractive, intelligent and proud, but her position as a 'kept woman' makes her an outcast from society. Many years later, in very different circumstances, the two men encounter Maria again and once more feel the power of this enigmatic woman who has indelibly marked their lives.

READ MORE IN PENGUIN

A CHOICE OF TWENTIETH-CENTURY CLASSICS

The Prodigy Hermann Hesse

Hesse's early novel *The Prodigy* is based on his own experiences of a narrow and uncaring education. Hans Giebenrath is a gifted child and the victim of provincial ambitions. Sent to theological school, the intelligent and imaginative boy is gradually driven to nervous collapse in a situation from which there seems to be no escape.

Something Childish and Other Stories Katherine Mansfield

'The singular beauty of her language consists, partly, in its hardly seeming to be language at all, so glass-transparent is it to her meaning. Words had but one appeal for her, that of speakingness' – Elizabeth Bowen

Collected Poems 1947–1985 Allen Ginsberg

Leading poet of the Beat generation, spokesman for the anti-war generation, an icon of the counter-culture, Allen Ginsberg remains an authentically American voice. This volume brings together four decades of bold experiment and provocative verse from *Howl*, one of the most widely read poems of the century, to his later, highly acclaimed collection, *White Shroud*.

Incest Anaïs Nin

Spanning the years 1932–4, the material in *Incest* was considered too explosive to include when the journals were originally published. In it, Nin reveals her incestuous affair with her pianist father, and recounts other relationships, loves and desires.

The Last Summer Boris Pasternak

Pasternak's autobiographical novella is a series of beautifully interwoven reminiscences, half-dreamed, half-recalled by Serezha, an intensely romantic young man and former tutor to a wealthy Moscow family. Here he broods over the last summer before the First World War, 'when life appeared to pay heed to individuals, and when it was easier and more natural to love than to hate'.

BY THE SAME AUTHOR

Watermark

Over nearly two decades, Joseph Brodsky, Nobel laureate, visited Venice, usually in winter, and from his experiences created a mosaic of prose pieces. Part confessional, part meditation on water and stone, past and present, *Watermark* captures the elusive spirit of the city it portrays.

'Succeeds in saying something new about Venice – no mean feat. His book adds some distinctive noise to the long celebration of the city's fabulous conjunctions of water and stone' – Barry Unsworth in the *Sunday Times*

'Some of Brodsky's finest writing yet, passages of golden brilliance' – James Wood in the *Guardian*

'*Watermark* is a gracefully idiosyncratic work, one that obliquely mingles the author's own self-portrait with that of "this Penelope of a city"' – James Marcus in *The New York Times Book Review*

Less Than One

Less Than One reveals Joseph Brodsky's remarkable talents as an essayist. In prose of striking subtlety and power, he offers uniquely penetrating appreciations of favourite writers: on Dostoyevsky and the development of Russian prose, on Auden and Akhmatova, Cavafy, Montale and Mandelstam. This recollection also includes evocations of his early life, profound reflections on tyranny and the nature of Evil, and illuminating meditations on Leningrad and Istanbul.

'*Less Than One* has the excessiveness, impatience and exaction of genius about it: essays which dare the grand style, bringing ardent intelligence to bear upon poetry, politics and autobiography' – Seamus Heaney in the *Observer*

forthcoming:

On Grief and Reason